LOCOMOTIVES

in detail

| BULLEID 4-6-2 | 1 | MERCHANT NAVY |

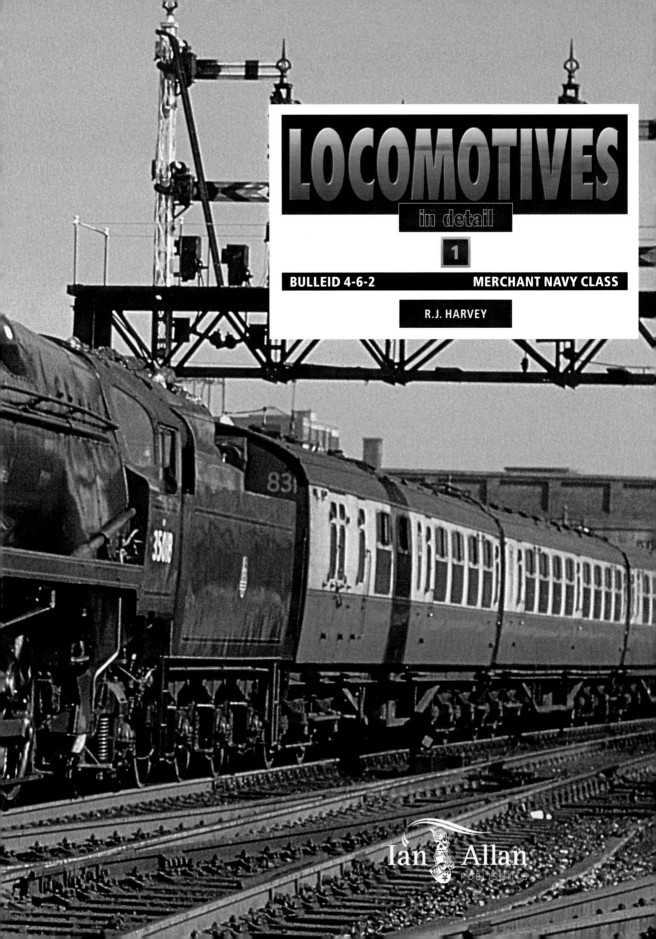

LOCOMOTIVES
in detail
1

BULLEID 4-6-2   **MERCHANT NAVY CLASS**

R.J. HARVEY

Ian Allan PUBLISHING

When Southern steam came to an end on British Railways (BR) in 1967, those who wished to perpetuate its memory by building Bulleid Pacifics in model form were often grateful to the late Albert Goodall, who introduced a series of photographically reproduced crests to complement a range of etched brass nameplates and other specialist components, thereby enabling an accurate finishing touch to models. Barry Fletcher, who had started recording in great detail aspects of BR (Southern) locomotive liveries in 1948 and who visited the Eastleigh paintshop on a number of occasions during the 1950s and 60s, worked with Albert to develop a deep understanding of the detail of Bulleid's locomotives, and some of the fruits of their endeavours have been incorporated into this book. To both Barry and to Shirley Goodall, I owe a large debt of gratitude. I am also indebted to Eric Youldon, who not only provided helpful information when plagued with a large number of tedious questions from me, but who also read drafts of the text and suggested several improvements.

In addition, the late George Woodward of Eastleigh was a most meticulous recorder of the railway scene and through the kindness of Tony Sedgwick, whose own recording started in earnest during World War Two, many week-ending dates when locomotives actually returned to service at Eastleigh shed after maintenance at the adjacent Works have been made available and have been incorporated into this work. I am also indebted to John Fry, Ken Rogers and John Sharpe of the Bulleid Society for the provision of information, to Southern Locomotives and the Swanage Railway for providing access to No 35027 for photography, and to the owners of photographic collections, who have kindly allowed their property to be reproduced herein. Grateful thanks are also due to Mr Richard Hardy, noted railwayman, writer and one-time custodian of several Bulleid Pacifics, with considerable 'sharp-end' experience, for approving my use of his words in the introduction and for adding useful points of interest.

Finally, thanks are due to Lin, who, after some 30 years of support for my interests and who probably knows far more about Bulleid's engines and carriages (and especially their appearance) than the average modeller, encouraged this book and, it is hoped, a fresh look at the subject.

R. J. Harvey, BSc, MBA, CEng, MIMechE
May 2004

Series Created & Edited by Jasper Spencer-Smith.
Design and artwork: Nigel Pell.
Cover design: Orbital Design Ltd, Bournemouth, England.
Produced by JSS Publishing Limited,
Bournemouth, Dorset, England.

Title spread: No 35018 *British India Line*, the first 'Merchant Navy' locomotive to be rebuilt. Southampton Central, March 1956. (CR/BS)

First published 2004

ISBN 0 7110 3013 8

Published by Ian Allan Publishing

an imprint of Ian Allan Publishing Ltd, Hersham, Surrey, KT12 4RG.

Printed by Ian Allan Printing Ltd, Hersham, Surrey, KT12 4RG.

Code: 0407/A2

Photograph Credits

Colour-Rail (CR) and their photographers
D. H. Beecroft (DHB); E. D. Bruton (EDB); G. S. Cocks (GSC); L. F. Folkard (LFF); H. J. James (HJJ); H. M. Lane (HML); P. Glenn (PGL); T. B. Owen (TO); W. Potter (WP); Friends of NRM (FNR); W. E. Robertson (WER); A. C. Sterndale (ACS); B. J. Swain (BS); Pursey C. Short (PCS); P. K. Tunks (PT); S. C. Townroe (ST); R. D. White (RDW). Photographs from other sources: ARS – Tony Sedgwick; AS/TT – Alec Swain/The Transport Treasury; CC – Colin Caddy Collection; ESY – E. S. Youldon Collection; GM – Gavin Morrison; HD/NS – Norman Simmons via Hugh Davies; HD/BB – Bob Barnard via Hugh Davies; IA – Ian Allan Library; LoS – Lens of Sutton Association; MP92½ – Milepost 92½; RAS – Rail Archive Stephenson; RCR – R. C. Riley; RCR/TT – R. C. Riley/The Transport Treasury; RKB/EWF – R. K. Blencowe Collection (the late E. W. Fry); RKB/SCT – R. K. Blencowe Collection (the late S. C. Townroe); RKB/WG – R. K. Blencowe Collection (the late W. Gilburt); RSC – R. S. Carpenter Collection; TCC – T. C. Cole.

All uncredited pictures from the author's collection.

INTRODUCTION

The number of alterations made to the 'Merchant Navy' locomotives created a complexity of locomotive classs possibly unsurpassed in Britain. However, a balanced view of the design must consider the Southern Railway's dramatically changing conditions and outlook between 1937 and nationalisation.

This book is intended for modellers, but it is also hoped that locomotive historians will find it of interest. Although the 'Merchant Navy' class totalled only 30 engines, they are among the most complex of any when all details are considered. Since a model constructor is primarily concerned with the external appearance of a locomotive at a point in time, this book will therefore give little consideration to matters internal to the locomotive, but external features and alterations will be covered as fully as reasonably possible in the available number of pages.

In producing any information for modellers, there are two important prerequisites: photographs and drawings of the subject. Fortunately, many photographers were active during the lives of these locomotives (with the exception of the difficult wartime years of 1941-45) and a good record has been made available through the assistance of those who supply prints. A selection has been reproduced here. With regard to drawings (and it must be said that drawings of these locomotives hitherto published have not always been held in the highest regard by those with a specialist interest in them), it may come as a surprise to learn that the National Railway Museum (NRM) lists some 3,000 drawings for Bulleid's Pacifics among its collection. Unfortunately, it appears that the

Southern Railway (SR) did not produce any General Arrangement drawings for any of the batches of the 'Merchant Navy' (at least, none has come to light in the public domain), and so this writer is very grateful to Richard Green for preparing entirely new drawings in 4mm scale. As far as reasonably possible, profiles and dimensional information were derived from the official drawings with numerous supporting details obtained from 4mm drawings prepared by the late Albert Goodall and a great many photographs.

The appendices at the back of this book summarise the main external changes that took place, including liveries, with dates. It is hoped that these tables will provide easy reference for those who are concerned to produce models or layouts representative of a particular period in time. In the main, the dates are taken from the notebooks of the late George Woodward of Eastleigh. During the period of the Bulleid Pacifics, George recorded (on a week-ending basis) transfers of locomotives between Eastleigh Works and the shed for return to service. Whilst serving in the army until 1946, George retrospectively compiled his records using his 'contacts' and friends. Any missing dates have been obtained from other sources, such as Engine Record Cards (ERCs). Close comparison with such official records for many SR locomotives has proved to the satisfaction of

Left:
No 21C11 *General Steam Navigation* leaving Nine Elms shed in April 1947, shortly to back down to Waterloo. (CR/HJ)

Above:
An official view of
No 21C4 *Cunard
White Star* in
malachite green
livery probably taken
at the end of 1941
prior to the naming
ceremony. (SR)

the author that George Woodward's record is unsurpassed in its accuracy.

The Bulleid Pacifics have always seemed to be among those classes that polarise opinion. Maybe this was because of the startlingly novel appearance, so different from the conventional locomotive form as seen in the 1930s; maybe it was the brilliant shade of green with yellow lining that contrasted so strongly with sombre wartime austerity; maybe it was the sheer power, outclassing other Southern engines during World War Two on both freight and passenger work and all others in the 1948 locomotive exchange trials. For drivers, maybe it was this power combined with the relative comfort of the cab, the ride quality and the ease of preparation compared with many other classes that won favourable comment. On the other hand, maybe it was the difficulties with adequate smoke clearance and forward view that formed adverse opinions. For the shed staff, maybe it was the messy and difficult access inside the oil sump to maintain the valve gear, or the fiddling about with bolted covers on the casing that delayed access to valves and other components that created ill favour.

Whatever the deciding factors in people's minds, it seems to this writer that it is essential to understand the background against which Bulleid's mind conceived his Pacifics in the late 1930s. Sir Herbert Walker, General Manager of the Southern Railway from the Grouping in 1923 until 1937, may well have been alone among railway managers in this country in both appreciating the challenges facing the railways in those years and in really overcoming some of those challenges. Sir Herbert realised that the railway had to expand its traffic in order to retain and, if possible, improve its viability (there were government imposed caps on the fare structure and so on). He was prepared to reduce costs through rationalisation and, for example, to close branch lines for which no financially successful future could be envisaged. But to expand traffic and thus revenue, he realised that the Southern had to provide a good reliable service (including the provision of Pullman quality in certain cases) that passengers and freight users would want to use more and more, mainly against competition from road haulage although air travel was also beginning to have an effect. Electrification provided one way forward and the expansion of Continental traffic (mainly through the Port of Dover) and Intercontinental traffic (through Southampton) were others, and

of course, punctuality of the service was extremely important.

But, by 1937, the Southern Railway Board was not in favour of new major electrification schemes (the Board had recently refused to electrify the line through Tonbridge to Hastings). R.E.L. Maunsell, Chief Mechanical Engineer was shortly to retire, and so a new Chief was required to further the need for continued progress with attractive, reliable services without the benefit of electric power. Walker selected O.V. S. Bulleid, then assistant to Sir Nigel Gresley on the LNER, for the task. In striving for improvement, Bulleid seems to have left no stone unturned within his compass of responsibility: 'Last Giant of Steam' is not an undeserved title.

Design work for new steam power with both passenger and freight capability was well in hand before the outbreak of war in September 1939, but the poor availability of some materials influenced completion. Chain driven valve gear was substituted for gear driven. Bulleid was one of the pioneers of welding and the 'Merchant Navy's' welded steel firebox was a novelty in this country and saved the use of imported copper. The tender tanks also featured welding, but with this method of fastening in its infancy, combined

with the use of $^3/_{16}$in plate, the first design suffered badly, especially during early years of service. Also, the coupling rods needed replacing with higher quality steel during British Railways days.

The design, of course, was for an express passenger locomotive, but that does not mean that the locomotives had no freight capability. Far from it — it was not only during the wartime years that they were heavily used on freight work. During 1950 (when the practice of changing engines on most trains at Salisbury ceased) several 'Merchant Navy' engine workings were arranged to work express passenger trains from London to Exeter or *vice-versa* and to work freight or perishable traffic, for example milk, overnight in the opposite direction. The 'Equivalent to Loaded Goods' wagon limits each side of Honiton tunnel (the most severe section between London and Exeter) as set down in the 1947 Working Time Tables was 51 down and 54 up for an 'A' power class locomotive (Classes H15, N15/'King Arthur', 'Lord Nelson' and S15), but the 'Merchant Navy' was allowed five more wagons than this for loose-coupled services and up to 70 in total depending on the number of vacuum-fitted wagons at the head of the train.

Above:
No 21C15 at Bournemouth Central with nameplates boarded over prior to the naming ceremony. Note the missing door over the whistle valve and the absence of a grab handle on the smokebox door.

9

Above:
No 35028 *Clan Line* on an up excursion leaving Herne Bay, Kent. Note the Pullman car *Chloria* for HRH Princess Elizabeth, 6 July 1951.
(P. Ransome-Wallis)

For those who would like to find out more about the background to the 'Merchant Navy' class, the following bibliography provides useful historical and performance related information.

The Bulleid Pacifics of the Southern by C.J. Allen and S.C. Townroe, first published by Ian Allan as long ago as 1951, still provides a good background and is well illustrated. Also, *Bulleid of the Southern* by H.A.V. Bulleid (Ian Allan, 1977) provides a fascinating insight into aspects of Bulleid's career and work. *The Locomotives of the Southern Railway* part 2 by D.L. Bradley (Railway Correspondence and Travel Society, 1976) for many years provided the definitive work on Bulleid's Pacific locomotives. This is still useful, but has effectively been superseded by *Bulleid Power*,

The 'Merchant Navy' Class by A. J. Fry (Alan Sutton, 1990) especially for accuracy of detail. *The Book of the 'Merchant Navy' Pacifics* by R. Derry (Irwell Press, 2001) is also recommended, particularly for those who like to study lists of information such as provided by the Engine Record Cards. Both of these books are very well illustrated. Two papers on the subject of the introduction of the 'Merchant Navy' class are worth the effort of finding: *Attempts to Torpedo the Merchant Navy Class* by D.W. Winkworth, and *More Light on the Bulleid 4-6-2s* by Philip Atkins in the magazine *Railways South East* Winter 1990/1 and Winter 1991/2 cover the political machinations that took place against the background of wartime emergency. *Bulleid's Pacifics* by D.W. Winkworth (George Allen and

Unwin, 1974) is primarily concerned with performance in daily service and for this purpose is unparalleled. *Bulleid Pacifics at Work* by Colonel H.C.B. Rogers (Ian Allan, 1980) provides a British Railways slant on the subject, which to this writer is overly concerned with those difficulties of the original design, which had largely been overcome by the time the rebuilding operation was instituted. Rogers overlooked the feelings of the passenger who, having purchased a ticket, simply wanted the engine at the head of the train to get to the destination on time: this passenger was not concerned if the fireman shovelled a little more coal in order to meet the train's demands for power or whether the locomotive was out of service for an extra day whilst fitting staff made sure it was good for service; the knowledgeable

passenger felt that his prospects of a right time arrival were better with a Bulleid Pacific at the head than with many other types of engine.

As a final comment in this brief overview we may turn to a noted railwayman trained on the LNER, who, for a period in the 1950s, was shedmaster at Stewarts Lane, where three 'Merchant Navy' class and 16 of the Bulleid Light Pacifics were based. Mr R.H.N. Hardy, writing about his personal experiences with these engines, commented thus: 'Bulleid…was not particularly concerned with the reaction of those poor souls who had to maintain his machinery. But just as it was our job to run the railway with what we were given, it was also our job to master the eccentricities of a wonderful machine' and he continued about the performance of the smaller, lightweight 'West Country' class even when the fireman was struggling for steam on a day when the engine was not at its best (while readers should remember that the main differences between the 'Merchant Navy' and the lightweight version were that the former had larger, 18in cylinders and a larger grate): '…a "West Country" with three $16^{1}/_{2}$in x 24in cylinders could just about time a 450-ton boat train up from Dover with no more than 160–180psi in the boiler. By hard work and enginemanship it could be done… But how could those little cylinders find the power to do the job when the LNER 'A4s', marvellous engines with larger cylinders, were poor tools for the job in such conditions?' Clearly, not all of Bulleid's ideas for reducing maintenance worked out in practice, but to overlook the commendation 'wonderful machine' would be extremely neglectful.

However, we must move on to consider the locomotive that emerged from Eastleigh Works and undertook its first main line test run on 18 February 1941. No 21C1 was the first of 10 authorised under order No 1068, collectively known as the first series. A second batch of 10 (the second series) was constructed under order No 1189, starting in 1944. These incorporated alterations deemed necessary as a result of experience with the earlier engines. A final batch of 10 (the third series) was started under order No 3393 in 1948 and included further alterations. All of the engines were constructed at Eastleigh Works with tenders for the first and second series constructed at Ashford Works and for the third series at Brighton Works.

Left:
 The boiler backplate of No 21C1 in March 1941 as originally completed, with a regulator handle on the fireman's (right hand) side, an arrangement not perpetuated.
The position of the vacuum brake valve does little for the driver's forward view. (SR)

CHAPTER ONE

THE EARLY YEARS

The first series of 10 locomotives was built in 1941 and 1942.
Difficulties with smoke clearance and piston-valve rocker shaft
failures soon materialised and significant improvements were made,
but the smoke problem was never completely solved.

onsideration had been given to naming the locomotives after British victories of World War Two, but in the event, the names of shipping companies using the Southern's Southampton Docks were used.

No 21C1, *CHANNEL PACKET* AND No 21C2, *UNION CASTLE*, 1941

Named at Eastleigh on 10 March 1941, No 21C1 was coupled to 5,000-gallon tender No 3111. The locomotive was finished in matt malachite green with three horizontal yellow lining stripes. Cast gunmetal plates stating 'Southern' ownership were affixed to the tender sides and, in inverted horseshoe form, to the smokebox door. Cast number plates were positioned on the cab sides and on the sloping platework fitted above the buffer beam.

A number of difficulties manifested themselves at an early stage. Smoke clearance problems were immediately apparent[1] and were probably the most intractable: the comparatively narrow slot provided in front of the chimney to lift the exhaust seems to have been particularly ineffective (shown on Drawing E32327, which

[1] See, for example, the 1942 photograph of 21C8 on page 24, which although with alterations to the casing around the chimney still suffers smoke clearance problems.

also shows the cover for the chimney and which was also soon abandoned). The tender soon showed defects in the welding. Photographs show that the roof casing at this stage had a very plain appearance: three holes sufficed for the safety valve tops to show through; the whistle also had a circular hole for its emissions; the whistle valve and steam manifold valve had no obvious easy means of access.

Accordingly it was found possible to make a limited number of alterations to No 21C2 before this was released from Eastleigh Works in June 1941. These alterations included an increase in the size of the clean air collecting aperture above the smokebox door and the slot in front of the chimney was abandoned in favour of a much larger rectangular opening delivering the clean air all around the chimney. A footstep was provided on the front right-hand side buffer as well as left-hand side, the front numberplate was lowered to the vertical surface immediately above the bufferbeam and lamps and lampirons were moved up. The engine undertook its trial trips in plain malachite green livery coupled to tender No 3112. Yellow lining was added before the naming ceremony on 4 July 1941.

Both of these engines were found to be considerably overweight and further alterations were incorporated into the building of the third locomotive. The tables for 21C1 and 21C2 show

Left and below:
No 21C1 photographed in May 1941 by the late S.C. Townroe. The right-hand side slidebars and crosshead are seen (left) and the oblique view of the front (below) shows the inverted horse-shoe, repositioned front numberplate and bottom row lamps. Also visible on the angled plate above the number-plate are the catches which secured the hinged footplating below the smokebox door. Below this footplating were the lubricators and steam generator. (RKB/SCT)

Left:
Tender No 3111 attached to No 21C1 around March 1941. Note the footsteps and handrails carried over from Maunsell's designs, but soon rejected in favour of tubular ladders.

Far left:
A portrait of No 21C1 *Channel Packet* at Eastleigh in 1941 after the initial alterations.

Left and far left:
No 21C1 *Channel Packet* photographed during March 1941, showing the profile of the locomotive as originally conceived by Bulleid and the style of the name, number and ownership plates. (SR)

Right:
No 21C7 at Dover
shed in October
1944, whilst
engaged in trial
workings on the
Eastern Section.
Note the original
arrangement of the
raves at the rear of
the tender.

the dates when other notable alterations were made to bring these engines to a nominal 'standard' for operational purposes. It should be noted that certain details of these two locomotives, in particular the casing, remained unique among the class and photographs should be followed for detailed information.

FIRST SERIES TENDERS, 1941-45

The underframe of the first series tenders was based on the 'Schools' class design. To this Bulleid added his own design of body. The sides in cross-section were given a radius of 22ft and were made of $^3/_{16}$in steel plate (8ft and $2^5/_8$in at the base of the skirting, 8ft and 5in wide at the floor plate, 9ft at the widest point, drawing No E31341) but there were several Maunsell details, especially on the first three, Nos 3111-3. Notice the rear of tender No 3111 (see page 17), especially the high raves completely enclosing the space above the tank top, the footsteps and handrails on the rear panel and a single short ladder below the buffer beam. The high-mounted vacuum brake hose connection was soon altered to a lower position at the base of the bufferbeam. Drainpipes were provided down through the tank to allow any overflow from the filling operation to escape. Electric lighting (but not

yet the coupling lamp) is evident. Bulleid also provided water fillers on each side at the front, in the cab, but these were found to be more of a liability than an asset and became fixed out of use until being removed in the early 1950s. Tender Nos 3113-20 had blackout slides fitted at the cab end cutaway.

The arrangement of the cab end of the tender proved unsatisfactory and revised arrangements were made for housing the fire irons and an additional locker was provided. The bulkhead was repositioned so that there was no overall loss of coal space.

On tender No 3114 and subsequent first series tenders, the footsteps and handrails on the tender rear panel were replaced by two tubular-steel ladders with three rungs each and the single short ladder below the buffer beam was replaced by a two-rung ladder situated below each buffer. A footblock was fitted to the top of the buffer housing.

After completion of these first series tenders and in the light of experience with the locomotive where a wide range of traffic was being operated (eg fast passenger trains and heavy goods trains over the Waterloo-Exeter main line) manually operated gravity sandboxes and delivery pipes were added below the fall plate. The delivery pipes directed the sand

under the tender wheels and although a definitive reason has not been found for this, such an arrangement is more appropriate as an aid to braking on the tender when working unfitted goods trains than for use on the locomotive driving wheels when running tender first.

After the war, the high rave at the rear of the tender was cut away and the ladders were altered to suit. In some cases it would appear that new ladders were provided, again with three rungs, but tenders Nos 3113 and 3117 were left with only two rungs, so the existing ladders may simply have been shortened.

Nos 21C3-10, 1941-42

In order to reduce the weight of the engines, the most obvious changes introduced with No 21C3 in September 1941 was the use of 'Limpet' board (an asbestos product) for the side casing and the use of painted tender ownership inscriptions and locomotive numbering. Drawing No E32647 ('Arrangement of Casing for Smokebox using "Limpet" sheets', 21C3 and future) shows that this was only ¹/₁₆in thick. The cast gunmetal ownership plate on the smokebox door was retained, but altered to a roundel: the former 'horseshoe' design was

made into a complete circle by adding a segment stating the place and the year of construction. The most noticeable feature of the limpet board casing was an external horizontal stiffening rib (effectively a 'box' section), arranged to coincide with the middle horizontal yellow line of the malachite green livery.

A less noticeable addition was a small window high up on the fireman's side, provided to illuminate the Detroit lubricator.

Nos 21C4–5 were completed to the same standard as No 21C3 and entered traffic in malachite green livery with yellow lining between December 1941 and January 1942. At this point the locomotives had sanding to the front of the centre driving wheels only and this proved inadequate. Nos 21C6 onwards had sanding added to the leading driving wheels. No 21C6 was completed in malachite livery but the completion of No 21C7 coincided with a high-level decision by the SR to cease using green paint for new locomotives and those requiring repainting. So although during construction No 21C7 received malachite green paint but no lining, it was repainted in black before entering traffic in June 1942. Nos 21C5 and 6 did not retain green livery very long, as they were both

Above:
No 21C3 *Royal Mail* photographed in works grey paint around September 1941 when 'sunshine' lettering (here in white and black) was new. The internal line applied to the 'C' of the number was a mistake, only the company title was normally given this feature. (IA)

repainted in black for the official naming ceremonies. Nos 21C8-10 were finished in black livery and entered traffic in the period June-July 1942.

FIRST SERIES ENGINES, 1942-45

Two major problems remained with these engines: poor smoke clearance with impaired visibility from the cab and breakage of the rocker shafts. The latter need not concern the modeller: the problem was identified as the omission of balance pipes between the ends of the valve chests. Being arranged for steam outside admission, under certain conditions very high differential pressures could arise between the ends of the chests causing excessive stress on the operating levers and shafts, eventually causing breakage.

The former problem is, however, worth covering in rather more detail, particularly where there is interest in why features of the prototype being modelled were arranged the way they were. In a paper presented to the Institution of Locomotive Engineers on 3 September 1941 by Mr H. Holcroft (Assistant to the CME, Southern Railway) with Mr Bulleid in the Chair, the development of smoke deflectors on the Southern was explained in detail. In essence, the problem first became severe with the 'King Arthur' class engines from

1925. The problem was that engines of increasing power output with large diameter boilers and smokeboxes necessarily were fitted with short chimneys so that they fitted the loading gauge. A soft, efficient exhaust from a short chimney could not clear the layers of stagnant air along the top and sides of the boiler that moved along with the locomotive, so smoke and steam were easily trapped within those layers. causing an obstruction to the driver's view. An acceptable, although not perfect, solution was derived as a result of trials with various devices fitted to locomotives in service. The Southern was the first company in this country to use smoke deflectors and the pattern fitted to many of Maunsell's engines became well-known. This device collected clean air in front of the smokebox and directed it along the sides of the boiler, so destroying the stagnant air pockets and providing a clear view for the driver (under most circumstances). In order to demonstrate that an optimal solution had been reached or to find further ways of improving matters, wind tunnel tests were carried out on models of the 'Schools' class 4-4-0s and a Maunsell 'U' class 2-6-0 in the early 1930s. In the event, a satisfactory compromise was considered to have been found.

In the discussion on Holcroft's paper, experience on the LNER was outlined and the findings from that company were that

Above:
No 21C5 *Canadian Pacific* photographed on 21 March 1942 having been repainted in black livery for the naming ceremony. (IA)

Left:
No 21C5 *Canadian Pacific*. Compare the front end appearance with No 21C1 on page 15, taken a year earlier. The enlarged aperture above the smokebox door, roundel and painted number are particularly evident. (IA)

streamlining materially benefited smoke lifting by carefully directing the air currents that flowed around the locomotive. The best results obtained had been with the design fitted to the 'A4' class locomotives. Bulleid's contribution at this meeting was to summarise the main findings and he added that engines of the day, particularly those with large chimneys and multiple jets, exhausted their steam at a pressure very little above atmospheric and so there was little energy left to clear smoke from the cab windows, particularly with modern high-pitched boilers. Further, Bulleid expressed his personal view that it might never be possible to prevent smoke drifting down on to a cab under all conditions, especially where a side wind was present, and he suggested that the problem was almost insoluble.

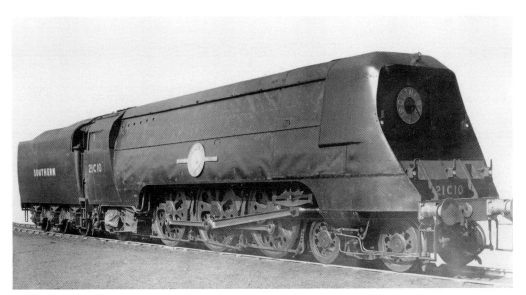

The foregoing therefore indicates two lines of thinking in Bulleid's mind. First, that streamlining offered a good if partial answer to a problem that could not be completely solved in locomotives of conventional arrangement. The second is that a complete solution could be achieved if the driver was positioned in front of the exhausting smoke and steam. Bulleid's direction is clear when the 'Leader' design is considered, but that is outside of the scope of this book.

So, with severe smoke clearance problems in 1942, Nos 21C6, 7 and 10 in particular received a number of modifications during the second half of 1942 and early 1943, the development of which were supported by wind tunnel tests using models. Firstly, the aperture in the roof casing around the chimney was increased in area

Above:
No 21C8 (un-named) at Surbiton on a down West of England train in the late summer 1942, a regular 'Merchant Navy' working at this time. Note that the exhaust pierces the haze of smoke hanging in front of the chimney and along the top of the casing.

(shown on drawing No E32647), but this was not in itself successful because the quantity of air collected by the casing in front of the smokebox was too great and spillage around the front caused stagnant pockets along the sides, and these filled with steam. Alterations to the chimney lip were tried and No 21C7 was given trials with ugly smoke deflector plates fitted on the outside of the front casing.

The best improvement was found by altering what has become known as the 'widow's peak' into a cowling (drawing No W5815), or hood, whilst retaining the larger aperture in the roof casing around the

chimney and by providing smoke deflectors which 'flared-out' from the casing front and directed clear air along the sides towards the cab windows (drawing No E34272). This overcame the 'air spillage' problem with the original design. A disadvantage was that the flared-out deflectors themselves slightly reduced forward visibility, but these changes were made during 1943 and 1944 to all of the first series engines.

With regard to sandboxes and delivery pipes, sanding was added to the rear driving wheels in 1943-46, and all first series engines were brought to the same standard.

FIRST SERIES TENDERS, 1946-51

Around 1948, an electric light and switch unit to illuminate night-time coupling operations was fitted close to the centre of the rear panel. Also in 1948, tender No 3115, coupled to Engine No 21C5/35005, was fitted with mechanical stoking equipment. The screw feeder took up water space, and to compensate the tender tank was made higher behind the coal-bunker. The ladders were also made higher to suit and had an extra rung, making four rungs in total. After the conclusion of the trials with the mechanical stoker in April 1951, the equipment was

removed and at some point the tender water tank was altered back to standard.

Now, a decade after the end of the 1940s, electric arc welding was commonplace and, for example, riveted construction began to look antiquated. But in the early 1940s on the railways of this country welded steel fireboxes were a novelty, which Bulleid helped to promote. There were many advantages but there was also one particular difficulty, of which the fastidious modeller needs to be aware. Although the larger watering sites had been equipped with softening plant for many years, in order to reduce corrosion of the firebox and further reduce scale

Above:
No 21C12 *United States Lines* on 25 May 1945 near Winchfield. The cowl design has cleared any smoke from in front of the chimney and the casing sides are also clear, but the vulnerability of the deflector-mounted headcode disc can be appreciated.

Above:
No 21C1 *Channel Packet* at Salisbury on 26 September 1946 with fairing behind the chimney and showing how the flared-out smoke deflectors of the first series were set in relation to the front edge of the cowling. (RCR/TT)

Right:
No 35005 *Canadian Pacific* with mechanical stoker at Clapham Junction on 13 August 1949, showing how the tender tank top was raised in height to compensate for the water capacity lost by the coal feeder. The ladders have four rungs. (Courtesy R.M. Casserley)

build up, Bulleid turned to French experience after the war and introduced to the SR a water treatment system known as TIA. This was in addition to existing water treatment facilities installed at major locations. The problem did not affect copper fireboxes in quite the same way, and was more severe with certain waters than others, in particular those supplies which came from areas of chalk in the counties to the east of Devon. Locomotives based at Exmouth Junction were less badly affected and so the priority for installation was directed towards those operating to the east.

The TIA (*Traitement Intégral Armand*) system essentially consisted of a container (to hold the liquid chemicals) and pipework fitted on top of the tender tank between the rear of the bunker and the water filler. Steam heating was provided (this was the small vertical pipe adjacent to the fireman's side ladder on the rear panel) and an 'air' pipe was fitted from the top of the container and down into the tender tank. Modellers may note that this air pipe (of inverted 'U' form) was vulnerable and became protected by a piece of sheet steel again of inverted 'U' form. When the tender was low in water, the air pipe became empty of water, so that when the fireman replenished the tender the rising water level slightly pressurised air that remained in this pipe. This slight air

pressure was imparted to the container and forced a volume of chemical into the tender tank. By this means, each time the tender was replenished. an approximately proportionate amount of chemical 'dose' was added to the water. The chemicals used were under the control of qualified staff based at the major sheds. For example, at Stewarts Lane in the mid-1950s there was a Water Treatment Controller and three 'Blowdown' men working round the clock: they blew down the Bulleids after every trip (blowing down 'on the road' had ceased by this time) and controlled the chemicals. Blowing down of the boiler at regular intervals removed any sludge, and the intervals between boiler washouts were substantially increased to 56 days. In order to accommodate the rather bulky TIA container, the auxiliary vacuum reservoirs required re-arrangement into a pyramid form. During 1956 or possibly shortly before and applicable to each of the three series of tenders, a self-explanatory 'TIA In Use' notice was displayed in the centre of the rear panel by means of a holder attached to the horizontal electrical conduit just to the left of the junction box, between the ladders. The notice itself was of 'L' section and with the base secured in the holder, the upright stood out at right angles to the rear panel, and, written on both sides, was visible from both ladders.

Above:
No 21C4 *Cunard White Star* at Eastleigh on 25 May 1946. Note the flared-out smoke deflectors with cowling above, a fairing behind the chimney and hinged cover for the whistle valve. The lamp irons have been moved to the smokebox door: No 21C4 was possibly the first to receive this alteration.
(G. O. Pearce)

SECOND SERIES LOCOMOTIVES

The second series of 10 was built in the years 1944 and 1945.
Experience with the first series enabled a number of improvements
and some simplifications of form to be incorporated into the design.

The Southern was pleased that it had a locomotive capable of prodigious feats of performance and a second batch of 10 'Merchant Navy' class locomotives was authorised by Order No 1189.

Nos 21C11-20, 1944-45

Although similar to the first series as they had been developed up to 1944, there were a number of differences which affected the detailed appearance, some very subtle. Since the 'widow's peak' had, perforce, been changed to a hood (the railway referred to this as 'Front End Cowling', drawing No W5815) the front casing was reworked. Whereas in the first series design the locomotive plan view showed a gradual tapering inwards in width in front of the cylinders with the side casing formed partly on top of the buffer-beam, the second series had no such taper but curved sharply inwards from the width of the cylinders to meet the bufferbeam, not on top, but to its rear. The drawings in the Appendix show this detail. As a result, the angled plate across the front of the locomotive above the bufferbeam no longer required angled ends but could be made of rectangular platework. The smoke deflectors were of similar size to the first series type that 'flared-out' from the original front edge of the casing, but had no flaring and presented less of an obstruction to the forward view from the cab. Because the casing front edge was slightly further back, the front edge of the smoke deflectors was further back when compared with the front edge of the cowling.

Regarding the cab, the front edge no longer had a forward curve in the side elevation as in the first series, but was made vertical. The height of the cab roof and the rear boiler casing did not taper down as the first series had done, and at the rear of the cab a screen was provided with a window, each side, to reduce draughts.

The curved ends of the cut-out above the driving wheels on the first series were not continued: at the front the cut-out was right-angled and at the rear a straight slope. The contours of the tender were also changed. No 21C18 was fitted with driving wheels that were fabricated from steel sections rather than cast as a whole. The appearance of these wheels was broadly similar to the standard Bulleid 'Boxpok' type, but they do not appear to have been successful because they were replaced (from photographic evidence probably in May 1949) by the cast type and the experiment was not repeated. Forward sanding was provided to all driving wheels on second series locomotives when built.

Above:
No 21C18 *British India Line* at Raynes Park with a down Bournemouth/Weymouth train, May 1946.
(CR/EDB)

Left:
No 21C7 *Aberdeen Commonwealth*, one of the last to lose wartime black for malachite green, with the 12.50pm Waterloo-West of England express, probably in the late summer of 1947.
(R. F. Dearden)

Right:
Right:
The rear of the
tender of No 21C11
*General Steam
Navigation* at Nine
Elms in 1946. Note
that the coupling
light has not yet
been fitted.

Right:
The cast trailing
truck of No 21C11.
(AS/TT)

Above:
No 21C11 *General Steam Navigation* on Salisbury shed, 26 September 1946. Note the unique bulbous casing in front of the cylinders. It is fitted with short smoke deflectors and in clean black livery except for the firebox casing which appears to have been stained by water deposits. (RCR/TT)

Left:
The left-hand cylinder slidebars, crosshead, bogie and front driving wheel of No 21C11. The open access door to the front sandbox can be seen, also the sand-delivery pipe at the wheel. (AS/TT)

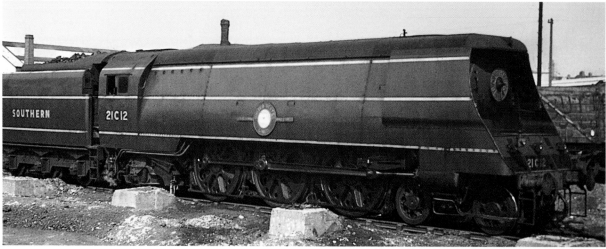

SECOND SERIES TENDERS
Nos 3121-30, 1944-51

The tender tank was made from $^1/_4$in plate, an increase from the first series and the sides in cross-section were formed from a composite of 22ft, 50ft and 17in radii (the latter at the raves), giving a maximum width of 9ft (NRM/Eastleigh drawing No W4885) and 5,100 gallons capacity. The sides of the coal bunker also curved inwards at the top. The space between the coal bunker and the side raves was utilised for fire iron storage and a glass spectacle was fitted at the cab end to aid tender-first running. The rear ladders again had three rungs, but the tops of the stiles

were fitted with returns and were welded near the top of the rear panel. The lower short ladders were suspended from the bufferbeam and framing, with an additional support from the guard iron. There was no skirt as such, just a mere $^1/_2$in overlap of the floor plate to facilitate welding, so the steam and vacuum pipes were visible along the top of the frames.

The frames were similar to the first series, and although drilled for the long spring suspension links, conventional hangers were fitted. These tenders were built with the sandboxes that had been retrospectively fitted to the first series.

When TIA water treatment was fitted, the vacuum reservoirs on top of the tender tank

Right:
No 21C18 at Bournemouth Central late in 1945, in malachite green but with nameplates boarded over prior to the naming ceremony. Note the fabricated-type driving wheels and as-built short smoke deflectors.(CC)

Below:
No 21C18 now named *British India Line* at Bournemouth Central on 30 June 1946. Note the rearwards extension to the smoke deflectors. The fairing behind the chimney can just be seen.(CC)

were, like the first series, rearranged into a pyramid and the TIA compound container was positioned on the right-hand side (NRM/Eastleigh drawing No E43245 shows this). The pipe visible alongside the right hand ladder on the tender rear panel was to provide steam to the TIA tank, and there was also a heater drain pipe into the tender. It is also worth noting that the Eastleigh drawing shows that the top of the tender tank on this series could have a camber, presumably to allow water spillage to run to the drains at the sides, as a note on the drawing states that the TIA container might require a pad welded 'to tender top plate (when necessary) to ensure that container is level'.

FIRST AND SECOND SERIES ENGINES, 1946-47

Although the early problems with smoke clearance had been significantly reduced (see the photograph of No 21C8 on page 24) side winds could still create difficulties and work continued to see whether matters could be

further improved. Observations and tests took place with locomotives in traffic, and further wind tunnel tests were conducted.

No 21C18 appeared in June 1946 with a small rearwards extension of the smoke deflectors, but a further improvement was found as a result of making the smoke deflectors not only longer, but deeper (drawing No W7396 'Wing Plate'.) No 21C18 appeared thus when it worked the first post-war 'Bournemouth Belle' in October 1946, and No 21C4 had a similar design (but necessarily adapted at the leading edge to fit the taper of the front casing) when it worked a special train to Southampton in connection with the Cunard-owned liner *Queen Elizabeth*. The others were similarly equipped during the course of the next few months, some apparently 'on shed' using new parts supplied from Eastleigh. It is worth noting that only engines equipped with the new and larger smoke deflectors could carry the 'Devon Belle' side wings, and in order to carry these wing-shaped nameplates a batten to retain the top edge was fixed to the deflectors.

Also in this period, reportedly because the route indicating discs could be blown off

Above:
No 21C15 *Rotterdam Lloyd* at Bournemouth Central probably during the summer of 1946. Compared with the earlier photo on page 9, the engine has a grab handle and disc brackets on the smokebox door.

Above:
No 21C2 at Exeter Central in the latter part of 1947 or early 1948. The locomotive has a Flaman speed recorder, originally fitted in 1945 for trials on the Eastern Section prior to the reintroduction of the 'Golden Arrow'. The fairing behind the chimney has been removed. (IA)

Above:
A tender end view of
No 21C1 *Channel Packet*,
circa 1947. Compare with
the 1941 photograph of
tender 3111 (see page
17): the rear raves have
been cut away; the
tubular-steel ladders have
three rungs; the coupling
light is not yet fitted. (LoS)

Left:
No 21C11 *General Steam
Navigation* at Clapham
Junction with the down
'Devon Belle', August
1947. Five sets of
headboards were
required when the train
ran in both directions on
the same day. In this
period, the train name on
the Waterloo-Wilton
section appears to have
been written in white
lettering but elsewhere,
cream lettering was in
evidence. (CR/HJ)

the bracket on the smoke deflector leading edge under adverse conditions caused by wind or a passing train, these disc brackets were removed from above the lamps to a new position on the smokebox door. No 21C4's record card includes the note 'Head Code boards on Smokebox door fitted to Drg – 27/4/46' and this may have been the first locomotive so modified. All engines were quickly so fitted. Notice that in some areas, railwaymen referred to the route indicating discs as 'boards', or 'head-boards', elsewhere 'disc-boards', although in the SR official 'Engine Head Signals' booklets, the instructions referred to the positioning of the 'disc-shaped white boards' for a particular route. A further advantage of this disc repositioning was that when, for example, the Waterloo-Bournemouth code was displayed, the upper of the two boards no longer infringed the driver's visibility.

Nos 21C1-15 had been built without a grab handle on the smokebox door, but Nos 21C16-20 were so fitted during construction. Nos 21C11-15 were soon equipped, but strangely, some of the first series never were until rebuilt. Bradley states that No 21C7 was the only member of the first series to have been fitted, but Nos 35004-5/8 also received them during the years shortly before rebuilding, according to photographs.

During 1947, it was felt that some improvement would be made to lifting the locomotive exhaust clear of the casing roof if the fairing behind the chimney was removed. Consequently, these fairings were removed as the engines passed through works, but by around 1950 it was decided that there was no material benefit and so they were replaced and few were without them by the end of 1953. The matter was never, however, satisfactorily resolved one way or the other and in the late 1950s the fairings were once again removed, but few of the 'Merchant Navy' class were affected by this time because of the rebuilding programme.

Far left above:
No 21C16 *Elders Fyffes* photographed in November 1945 painted in black livery. (RAS)

Far left below:
No 21C17 *Belgian Marine*, with standard-length smoke deflectors and 'Devon Belle' battens, here with the Southern Railway's 'The Bournemouth Belle' headboard, at Bournemouth West, 4 October 1947. (SLS)

Left:
No 21C18 *British India Line* photographed in 1946 during the short period when an extension had been added to the original smoke deflectors.

CHAPTER THREE

AFTER NATIONALISATION

The effects of nationalisation were most apparent with
rapidly changing liveries, but further improvements were made.
The third series of 10 locomotives was built in the years 1948 and 1949.

Both first and second series engines were now dominating the Southern's Western Section expresses and there was a will to demonstrate their capability to the newly nationalised railway.

FIRST AND SECOND SERIES ENGINES, 1948-51

The Southern prepared Nos 35017/35019/ 35020 for the 1948 locomotive exchange trials against a background of some continuing concern at the difficulties with smoke clearance from around the sides of the boiler and cab under certain conditions. Of these three, No 35020 alone was provided with a further rearwards extension to its smoke deflectors in May 1948, but in the event was kept as reserve engine and did not actually participate in the trials. These smoke deflectors, unique to the class, were retained until rebuilding. For the period of the trials in May and June 1948, these three engines were paired with black-painted LMS tenders equipped with water pick-up apparatus. No 35018 also participated in the trials, but was limited to representing the class on the SR. All four engines were fitted with Flaman speed recorders for the trials.

The forward visibility problems due to poor smoke clearance were exacerbated by the small cab front windows. Glare and reflections from the footplate were also a problem with these windows. In August 1948, No 21C8 was fitted with new cab front windows arranged at an angle, to give what sometimes became known as a 'Vee' or 'Wedge' fronted cab. The existing two side windows were retained initially on No 21C8, but it was realised that if the two window arrangement was changed to three windows that could all slide, the crew could reach around to clean the front window. A further improvement for the first series engines introduced with the revised window arrange-ments was the provision at the rear of the cab of a turn-in to reduce draughts, as the second series had been built with. All other locomotives of the first and second series were altered to this same standard and No 21C8 received the three-window arrangement in July 1949.

Bulleid envisaged that the sandboxes of his Pacifics would be replenished using a flexible hose with the locomotive drawn up alongside a platform. Without such facility, the job became particularly difficult because of poor access due to the absence of a running plate on the locomotive. Particularly at the front sandbox, any sand that was tipped but did not enter the box could contaminate working parts such as the slidebars and crosshead. Of course, these parts were open to the elements and a small splasher had been provided to reduce contaminants being sprayed upwards from the rear bogie wheels and during

Right:
No 35017 *Belgian Marine*, seen here during the exchange trials, successfully restarted its train of 15 bogies on a 1 in 130 gradient, having been stopped by signals near Tebay. It was a feat which the LMR pilotman said its 'big 'uns' would not do.

Left:
No 35014 *Nederland Line* with modified cab and covered slidebars, still in malachite green, but renumbered and without inscription on the tender, circa 1949.
(J. H. Aston)

Left centre:
No 35015 *Rotterdam Lloyd* with modified cab and covered slidebars, still in malachite green, but renumbered and without inscription on the tender, 12 June 1949.
(RKB/WG)

Left bottom:
No 35009 *Shaw Savill* newly repainted in blue livery at Eastleigh, 4 September 1949. The original cab is retained but slidebar covers have been fitted. (RKB/WG)

Far left centre:
No 21C8 *Orient Line* with modified front cab window.
(L. Elsey)

Far left below:
Now renumbered and repainted, *Orient Line* has a fully-modified cab with three side windows and turn-in, Clapham Junction, 17 August 1949.
(TCC)

Right:
No 35017 *Belgian Marine* at Bournemouth Central in 1948, renumbered but otherwise in Southern Railway livery. (CR/HML)

Above:
No 35002 *Union Castle* at Nine Elms shed, 29 April 1950, repainted in blue but retaining the original cab. The rear of the tender shows the cut-down raves and coupling light.

Left:
No 35007 *Aberdeen Commonwealth*, 6 June 1950, at Exeter Central in British Railways blue livery. Note that there is no fairing behind the chimney. (CR/PT)

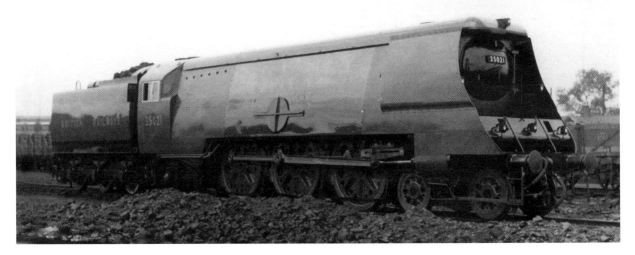

1949 a number of locomotives from the first and second series appeared with covers bolted onto the slidebars to help protect the working surfaces. Whether these covers caused lubrication problems, overheating of the crosshead due to the enforced absence of cooling air or were simply just a nuisance is not satisfactorily explained in the literature. However, the covers were removed from 1951.

Locomotives noted with these slidebar covers are Nos 35001/2/5/8–10/12/14–15/17–20. The covers were probably not fitted to Nos 35003/11/13/16 and the situation regarding Nos 35004/6/7 is unclear. The third series was not fitted with slidebar covers.

In September 1948, No 21C12 had had the leading sand pipes blanked off, but whilst the slidebar covers were considered to be a solution

further locomotives were not so treated. However, in June 1951 No 35019 had the sandboxes and piping removed from the leading coupled wheels and subsequently all engines of the class had the front sanding facility taken out of use and the access to the sandbox through the casing covered.

From about 1950, some of the second series locomotives received additional bracing of the leading edge of the smoke deflectors by means of a tie-bar affixed below and to the side of the smokebox door.

THIRD SERIES ENGINES
Nos 35021-30, 1948-51

The third series of 10 engines was built at Eastleigh in 1948-9. They were numbered to conform with

Left:
No 35025
Brocklebank Line at
Nine Elms, 1952.
Note (top) the
injectors and feed
pipework, damper
operating gear etc,
all on the fireman's
side, and (centre and
bottom) the ashpan
with dampers,
fabricated trailing
truck and steam
generator under
the driver's side
of the cab. (AS/TT)

Left:
No 35018 *British India Line* leaving Southampton Central, October 1949 with an up train. Note the top of the 5,100-gallon tender. (CR/WER)

Left:
Having settled the form of the blue livery, No 35024 *East Asiatic Company* is seen at Waterloo 21 June 1949 with a special train bound for Weymouth conveying members of the Royal Family. (CR/WER)

the British Railways system and given Nos 35021-30. In essence, they were identical with the second series to the standard of development as reached in 1948. All received the 'Vee' fronted cab with three side windows and screen at the rear, but none received the slidebar covers. A rather more subtle change was a new position for the Stone's generator. In the first series this had been hidden out of sight between the frames with the lubricators under the hinged platform in front of the smokebox door. The second series had the generator mounted under the cab floor, but hidden away behind the side sheeting. For the third series, the generator was lowered so that it was now visible below the cab side sheeting: see the close-up photographs of No 35025 (page 47).

THIRD SERIES TENDERS
Nos 3341-3350, 1948-51

These tenders followed the form of those built for the second series, but were increased in length to create a water capacity of 6,000 gallons. Improved internal bracing and welding techniques allowed a reversion to $^3/_{16}$in plate thickness for the sides. The relevant drawing (No E40454) indicates that the unusual wheelbase arose as a result of improvement to the balance of the axle loadings: 7ft 0in/7ft 4in. The extra length of these tenders provided more space at the rear on top of the water tank for the vacuum brake reservoirs and TIA equipment.

Left:
Fitting the 'Devon Belle' wings at Salisbury shed circa 1948. (RK/SCT)

Below:
No 35009 *Shaw Savill* near Sherborne on an up Waterloo train in 1950. Of interest is the absence of a fairing behind the chimney and the profile of the cowl against the lipped chimney and roof casing.

CHAPTER FOUR

THE EXPERIMENTAL ERA

The locomotive exchanges revealed a capability for high performance, but at the expense of relatively high coal, water and oil consumption. Availability was also considered low and a further tranche of modifications was carried out on selected engines.

By 1952, the number of days the Bulleid Pacifics spent out of service was still relatively high when compared with some other classes and a number of modifications was proposed for trial on a sample number of locomotives which have become known to some as the 'guinea pigs'.

FIRST, SECOND AND THIRD SERIES ENGINES, 1952-LATE 1950S

The most obvious external indication that a locomotive was one of the 'guinea pigs' was that the tender appeared with a new shape: essentially, the raves had been cut away (see below), and there were revisions to the livery. However, a number of less obvious changes were also instituted, some of which were not applied for evaluation on sample locomotives but were applied across the whole class during the course of the next two years or so. The tables on pp97–102 give dates of application of some of the alterations most significant to the model constructor.

Following the foregoing definition for a 'guinea pig' locomotive, 'Merchant Navy' No 35021 in February 1952 was the first to emerge from Eastleigh Works with a range of modifications. In addition to the tender, other external alterations included:

– Doors giving access to the manifold and whistle valves changed from hinged to sliding type;
– Revisions to the livery.

No 35012, in July 1952, received in addition, rather more extensive modification. From a performance point of view, the most significant alteration was a reduction in boiler pressure to 250psi. In practical operation, only rarely was it necessary for the regulator of a 'Merchant Navy' to be fully opened yet the class successfully worked its trains. Cost savings in boiler maintenance could be expected from a reduction in boiler pressure and this was the *raison d'être* for the change. Other external alterations included:

– New cylinder drains with two pipes of larger diameter;
– Removal of the casing in front of the cylinders to improve access and remove a tripping hazard.

In December 1952, No 35013 was also modified as a 'guinea pig', although the boiler pressure was not altered. No 35020 received the standard level of modifications in June 1952, but following its crank axle failure in 1953 it was given a general overhaul and left Eastleigh Works in July with modified cylinder

Above:
No 35015 *Rotterdam Lloyd* in standard blue livery at Branksome August 1952, prior to working the up 'Bournemouth Belle' from Bournemouth West to Waterloo. (CR/PCS)

Left:
No 35021 *New Zealand Line* at Eastleigh, 1 March 1952, newly released from the Works with cut-down tender and other 'guinea pig' modifications. (ARS)

Above:
No 35012 *United States Lines*, probably taken in July 1952. Note the 'spaced out' lining, hinged door at the manifold valve, modified cylinder drains and casing removed in front of the cylinders.
(Author's Collection)

Right:
No 35008 *Orient Line* at Clapham on 28 June 1952 with the 1pm Waterloo-West of England express. Note the fairing behind the chimney and hinged door at the manifold valve, but the casing ahead of the cylinders is still present.
(A. A. Sellman)

drains, a cut-down tender and modified livery, and so qualifies as a 'guinea pig'.

Further modifications introduced in this period included stronger coupling rods, firstly, it appears of a similar fluted pattern but in a higher-strength steel and later of a plain section. The caps that secured the coupling and connecting rods to the crankpins were designed for Bulleid by Mr R. Curl. The actual fastening was internal to the crankpin and this enabled a neat and slender external cap. Unfortunately, these caps reportedly gave difficulty when it was necessary to remove the rods and, sometimes, severe measures were accordingly required to effect the dismantling.

Accordingly, the main crankpin had the Curl fastening replaced by a washer, nut and locking pin to retain the big end. Later, this was replaced by a round cap secured with four studs with nuts, the latter being utilised for

securing the return cranks when locomotives were rebuilt. The Curl caps were retained for the leading crankpin on account of the restricted clearance behind the slidebars, but for the rear crankpin a small washer nut was permissible. It should be stressed that not all 'Merchant Navys' received all crankpin modifications before rebuilding: in fact, some received no modifications at all whilst in air-smoothed form.

When speedometers were fitted on the rebuilt locomotives from 1960, the drive was operated from the rear left-hand crankpin by means of a drive arm secured by four studs in place of the washer nut. Some of the engines rebuilt in 1959 received the four-stud retaining cap on this crankpin to facilitate the slightly later fitting of the speedometer.

Note that in the late 1950s, washout plugs were being provided on top of the front of the

Above:
No 35020 *Bibby Line,* 16 May 1954, retains the extra long smoke deflectors fitted for the 1948 exchange trials as well as the Flaman speed recorder drive bracket. However, the cut-down tender, sliding door at the whistle valve, modified cylinder drains, front casing removal and 'spaced' lining all indicate 'guinea pig' treatment. (RKB/EWF)

Left:
No 35004 *Cunard White Star* awaits the 'right away' at Waterloo around 1953. Note the open sliding door at the whistle valve, the modified cab and the Flaman speed recorder drive.

boiler just to the rear of the smokebox (previously it is understood that these were situated in the smokebox) and access covers were provided in the casing on any engines receiving boilers so fitted.

TENDERS, 1952-LATE 1950S

As a part of the 'guinea pig' trials four tenders, Nos 3342 (2/52), 3122 (7/52), 3124(12/52) and 3347 (6/53) appeared with a new shape in order to make easier the swinging of the 'bag' of a water column into the filler and to remove a feature which benefitted the aesthetic appearance of the locomotive but which trapped coal and water debris, suffered corrosion and required maintenance. Thus the raves were removed and also the fire iron tunnels were rearranged.

In addition, tender No 3343 was converted to be 'coal weighing' in July 1952 and, although

Above:
No 35026 *Lamport & Holt Line* at Victoria, 13 March 1955. The 5,100-gallon tender has the vacuum reservoirs stacked in a pyramid to provide space for the TIA container. (HD/NS)

Left:
No 35005 *Canadian Pacific* at Nine Elms, 6 September 1958. Compared with the photograph on page 26, the 5,000-gallon tender tank top has been lowered to the standard height and the lower side skirting has been cut away. The engine has plain coupling rods and the big end cap is secured by four studs with nuts. (RCR/TT)

reportedly photographed with No 35012, it emerged from Works behind No 35018. In 1956, it was decided to cut down all the Bulleid Pacific tenders and so the following were dealt with before the engines were rebuilt:

No 3111 (35001) on 6/56
No 3114 (35007) on 9/56
No 3121 (35011) on 8/57

When the 5,100-gallon second series tenders were 'cut down' alterations were made to the TIA system and vacuum reservoirs (Eastleigh drawing No E46505). The three vacuum reservoirs were replaced by two of 2ft 0in diameter positioned towards the right-hand side. The TIA container was moved across towards the left-hand side and its major axis arranged to be parallel with the vacuum reservoirs. A cover was now provided over the reservoirs and the

Above:
No 35024 *East Asiatic Company* at Exeter Central shortly after being repainted in BR green livery and before the 1952 alterations were commenced.

Right:
An interesting view of No 35020 *Bibby Line* in April 1953 shortly after a driving axle failure. The coupling rods and part of the brake gear have been removed and the failed wheelset has been secured clear of the rail. (RKB/SCT)

container, except that the end of the container with the filling lid was left protruding for purposes of access.

Around 1956, British Railways began to replace the TIA system with a simpler system that could be operated by the locomotive's crew. The chemicals were provided in the form of a solid briquette and placed into a circular feeder, which was much smaller than the TIA tank. At the base of the feeder in the tender tank, a tube with an adjustable number of holes (set by qualified staff to suit the locomotive's usual water supply), allowed the release of the chemicals. This feeder can still be seen on some tenders at the time of writing (eg No 3116) although the briquette system of chemicals has itself been superseded on some preserved railways and may no longer be used at all. During 1958, the presence of the BR system on a locomotive became denoted by a pale yellow circle painted on the cabside below the number (No 35030 in April 1958 may have been the first 'Merchant Navy' to receive this symbol). However, it was claimed that such a circle caused confusion with Western Region

route restriction codes and the water treatment circle was replaced by a yellow triangle! No 35028 was the first noted with the yellow triangle after a Works visit to Eastleigh, week ending 29 July 1961.

Also late in BR days before rebuilding, the side skirting of the 5,000-gallon first series tenders (which concealed on one side the vacuum pipework and on the other the steam heating pipework) was cut away and a programme of cutting down the raves of the tender commenced. This latter also involved alterations to the fire-iron tunnel, covers for the vacuum reservoirs and complete removal of the front water fillers and the provision of spectacle glasses for rearwards vision for the crew.

In British Railways days from around 1956 the ladders were altered so that each had only one high stile (to the outside, reformed from a semicircular top to a rectangular top, to act as a handrail) with the inner stile cut back to facilitate the fireman stepping across to the centre of the tender. At around the same time, the lower short ladders were removed from below the buffers and resited at the ends of the

Above:
No 35026 *Lamport & Holt Line* near Hildenborough, 23 July 1955. The view shows the resited safety valves. (SLS)

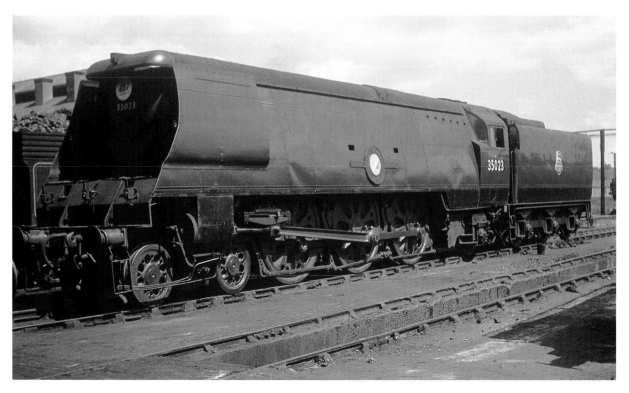

Above:
No 35023 *Holland Afrika Line* at Nine Elms, July 1956. (CR/PGL)

Right:
Tender 3345 was attached to No 35020 *Bibby Line* during the spring of 1956. The tender raves of the original design were painted black to accompany the rebuilt engine. The test cabling set up between a dynamometer car and the engine has been retained. Note the 'TIA IN USE' notice on the tender rear panel. (HD/BB)

Above:
No 35015 *Rotterdam Lloyd* at Eastleigh shed in May 1957 with the coal-weighing tender. (CR)

Left:
No 35020 *Bibby Line* with tender No 3345 for the trials of a rebuilt locomotive during the Spring of 1956. (IA)

Right:
No 35008 *Orient
Line* with the up
'Atlantic Coast
Express' at Sidmouth
Junction, May 1956.
Note the general
form of the front of
the locomotive. (IA)

bufferbeam/frames with an additional support from the guard iron to the lower rung. Also from about the same time, the long vertical links of the spring hangers were replaced by more conventional brackets.

British Railways removed the sandboxes from the tenders after the locomotives had been rebuilt as sand on the tender was seen as no longer necessary. By this time the quantity of vacuum-brake fitted freight stock available for the kind of fast overnight traffic to and

from the West Country that the 'Merchant Navy' class was being called upon to work had increased.

A further alteration which was applied upon rebuilding the locomotives was the provision of a BR-type standard water level indicator to the left of the brake handle (as one stands in the cab and looks to the rear). Previously, a very simple vertical tube with holes, supplied from the tank through a shut-off valve, provided indication.

Above:
No 35024 *East Asiatic Company* leaving Exeter Central with an up express, 29 June 1957. The safety valves are in the original position, but the casing around them has been altered to a 'well'.(RCR/TT)

CHAPTER FIVE

FURTHER ALTERATIONS

British Railways was still not happy with the costs associated with the operation of the Bulleid Pacifics and major redesign work was undertaken. All 30 of the 'Merchant Navy' class were rebuilt and given resemblance to the BR 'Standard' class.

The major features of the redesign involved the elimination of the chain-driven valve gear and oil bath, and the steam reverser.

THE REBUILT ENGINES, 1956-64

Whatever the arguments for or against the rebuilding of the 'Merchant Navy' class, the historical fact is that they were rebuilt between 1956 and 1959. The Appendix at the end of the book gives the relevant dates. Tenders, where not previously modified, were also treated. The only exception was in the case of No 35020, which was attached to an unmodified tender (No 3345) for purposes of trials between Waterloo and Exeter. The raves of this tender were used as a conduit for instrumentation cabling between locomotive and dynamometer car.

Both the accompanying photographs and the drawings show the totally different appearance of the rebuilt locomotives. Possibly the most obvious features are: the elimination of the Bulleid casing and replacement by conventional clothing; the provision of a running plate supported from the locomotive frames and thereby lower than the typical form used on locomotives of British Railways' design; and the provision of Walschaert's valve gear, the latter requiring major changes to the lubrication arrangements.

Less obvious changes included the cab roof, where previously the housings for the cab interior lights had protruded through, but now were mounted completely below the roof.

The first engine modified, No 35018, had a number of unique features and constructors of accurate models are advised to study photographs for the following: on the left-hand side the routing of the ejector pipe above the nameplate; sandbox fillers; position of mechanical lubricators. On the right-hand side, the routing of the twin boiler feed pipes and the sandbox fillers and the position of the mechanical lubricators were different from the others in the class. Further, the snifting valve (right-hand side) was hidden away by the smoke deflector but on the others this item was visible, the smoke deflector being cut away at the lower rear corner. Some of these variations were later changed to bring No 35018 to standard.

Later additions were of the BR form of Automatic Warning System (AWS) and Smith's Speedometers (see the tables).

One problem that arose with the rebuilt engines was that because of the retention of outside steam admission on the outside cylinders, when converted to conventional Walschaerts gear using a valve spindle and gland at the inner end of the valve chest, the forces on the piston valve heads created by the steam were no longer equal. There was no steam pressure acting over the area taken

Left:
No 35014 *Nederland
Line* working the
down 'Bournemouth
Belle' near Millbrook,
February 1957. (CR)

Right:
The first of the class to be rebuilt, No 35018 *British India Line* included a number of details that were subsequently changed. Within about two months, handrails were added to the smoke deflectors. It is working Duty 253 from Eastleigh shed. (RJH)

Above:
The same locomotive on Eastleigh shed, 14 April 1956. (RKB/EWF)

by the valve spindle and the effect was to push the valves back into the operating gear. This caused excessive wear and the remedy was to provide a spindle and gland at the outer end of the valve chest. However, the travel of this new spindle was sufficient to foul the angle in the running plate, between bufferbeam and smokebox.

No 35022 was the first to be so modified (in January 1958) and thimble type recesses or 'pockets' were built into the running plate to allow the new spindle to travel freely. The new gland required attention from time to time and access was found difficult (how many times have we heard that!) so three further varieties of 'pocket' were tried before a satisfactory solution was reached. First came a large hole in the angled running plate (entirely inside the

Left:
No 35009 *Shaw Savill* backs down to Exeter Central, 29 July 1958. Note the cut down 5,000-gallon tender including the TIA container and BR-type ladders. (RCR/TT)

smoke deflectors) which was protected by a step with a supporting valance. If the new gland was blowing, steam issued into the area between the smoke deflectors (not what smoke deflectors were intended for!). Nos 35005, 35019 and 35024 received this type of pocket (during 1959).

The second type converted the 'step' type of pocket into a small angular box, entirely inside the smoke deflectors. This solved the problem of steam issuing between the smoke deflectors, but access to the gland was difficult. This in turn led to a larger angular box being provided from 1962, protruding through the deflector platework and requiring the step outside the deflector on the angled footplating to be raised in position. All except No 35018 eventually received this large type of pocket.

Above:
No 35027 *Port Line* illuminated by a low sun at Eastleigh shed, 29 September 1961. (GM)

Above:
No 35020 *Bibby Line* on Salisbury shed for the 'road test' trials of 1956, coupled to the GWR dynamometer car. (CR/ST)

Right:
No 35017 *Belgian Marine* at Bournemouth West, with the 'Bournemouth Belle', 15 September 1964 . The locomotive has been fitted with large pockets and the AWS battery box is clearly visible above the bufferbeam. (GM)

Above:
No 35015 *Rotterdam Lloyd* ready to work the 'Golden Arrow' in 1959 complete with headboard and flags with the arrows mounted on the smoke deflectors. (CR/WP)

Right:
No 35022 *Holland America Line* at Eastleigh shed following a general overhaul, 4 August 1962. The locomotive has been fitted with large pockets and the AWS battery box and speedometer are clearly visible. (GM)

Right:
No 35023 *Holland Afrika Line* being serviced at Branksome, 9 September 1964. The large pockets are just visible. (GM)

Above:
No 35015 *Rotterdam Lloyd* leaving Gillingham (Buckhorn Weston) tunnel with the up 'ACE', probably in April 1960. (RJH)

Above:
No 35029
Ellerman Lines at
Bournemouth shed,
September 1960.
Note the small type
pockets, inside the
smoke deflectors.
(CR/DHB)

Right:
On 12 June 1967
No 35030 *Elder
Dempster Lines*,
without nameplates,
backs down from
Weymouth shed
towards the station
and shows useful
tender detail. Note
the Electrification
Warning Signs. (RCR)

REBODIED TENDERS

Because of the poor condition of a number of the first series tenders in particular, 10 new bodies were completed to a new design (drawing No E50504 of June 1958) at Ashford Works. Nine of these tenders had a nominal capacity of 5,250 gallons and suited either the 'Merchant Navy' or the smaller Light Pacific underframes. To achieve this, the tank sides (whose profile followed the original second series) were made higher so that the line of the fire-iron tunnel and tender rear was made into a continuous line (ie without the step down at the rear of the fire iron tunnel on the 'cut down' tenders). The vacuum reservoirs were 2ft in diameter and two were provided, completely covered by sheeting. A rectangular water filler was fitted in each rear corner of the tender top with the BR water treatment briquette carrier located between. A single ladder at the rear was provided for access to the tank top, with handrails positioned to aid the transition from the existing lower two-rung ladders suspended from the bufferbeam and frames.

Amendment 6 of drawing No E50504 (September 1961) called for replacement of the two fillers and single ladder by a single central filler and twin ladders in the event of renewals being needed, following traditional Bulleid practice, but it would appear that this change was never required. One new body was longer by some 2ft to replace the coal-weighing 6,000-gallon body of tender No 3343: it maintained this capacity and had the usual two rear ladders.

'Merchant Navy' tenders rebodied are as follows:

No 3111 (35001) on 2/63
No 3112 (35002) on 4/60
No 3115 (35005) on 5/59
No 3117 (35003) on 8/59
No 3118 (35018) on 1/62
No 3343 (35008) on 2/62

Later, No 3111 went to 35026 (4/65); No 3115 to 35014 (9/65); No 3118 to 35008 (10/64).

ENGINES & TENDERS, 1965-67

There were no further significant alterations to these locomotives and so this summary of the external modifications to Bulleid's 'Merchant Navy' class is effectively concluded. Steam working on the Southern region ended in July 1967. In the months leading up to this date, nameplates and smokebox numberplates were generally removed, usually for safe keeping by the owners. Several locomotives and tenders have entered the sphere of preservation, but further commentary is outside the scope of this book. It now remains to discuss some aspects of the liveries of the 'Merchant Navy' class.

Below:
No 35028, *Clan Line* at Nine Elms shed, July 1967, with a cut-down 6,000-gallon tender fitted with BR-type ladders and Electrification Warning Signs. (IA)

Right:
Rear of the tender of
Swanage Railway's
rebuilt 'Merchant
Navy' No 35027
Port Line. Note the
fire-irons tunnel
below the spectacle-
type window. (RJH)

Above:
The cab of No 35027 *Port Line* showing the motion lever control and also the vacuum brake valve. Note also the three sliding side windows. (RJH)

Left:
No 35027 *Port Line* in storage at Swanage, February 2004. The pressure gauges and water level gauges have been removed for security. Note the steam manifold and valves, (RJH)

Right:
The steam generator
on No 35027 *Port
Line* at Swanage in
February 2004. (RJH)

Below:
No 35027 *Port Line*
at Swanage in
February 2004,
showing the
speedometer drive
crank and flexible
connection. (RJH)

CHAPTER SIX

LIVERIES

There is no doubt that the Southern appreciated the value of publicity and Bulleid's strikingly modern design created much goodwill, particularly when set against 1940s austerity. Nationalisation and standardisation, however, brought more sombre tones.

The use of malachite green as the Southern's passenger locomotive colour had been finalised in 1940. To this bright bluish green, Bulleid added strong yellow horizontal lines to complement the profile of his new locomotives.

1941-45

No 21C1 was finished in matt malachite green with three horizontal yellow lining stripes; the rear of the tender was unlined green. Cast gunmetal plates stating 'Southern' ownership were affixed to the tender sides and, in inverted horseshoe form, to the smokebox door. Cast number plates were positioned on the cab sides and on the sloping platework above the buffer beam, the position of the latter being altered at an early stage. No 21C1 was to retain this livery until December 1943, when it was repainted black.

No 21C2 was painted for running trials in plain malachite green livery, but yellow lining was added before the locomotive's naming ceremony. No 21C2 was to retain this green livery until June 1944.

To reduce weight, Nos 21C3-10 were completed as follows: the cast tender ownership and the number plates were abandoned but the gunmetal ownership plate on the smokebox

door was retained. This was altered to a roundel by adding a segment stating the place and the year of construction to the original design. On locomotives finished in green, the horizontal stiffening rib built into the limpet board casing was used to coincide with the middle horizontal yellow line of the malachite green livery, the line thus being lowered when compared with 21C1, and was no longer cut by the cab windows. The lower line was also repositioned approximately 2in closer to the cut-out above the driving wheels, and green paint still showed below the yellow. The nameplate was positioned approximately centrally between the two lower lines, the distance from the edge of the nameplate to the edge of the lining being about $1^1/2$in. Note that the surround to the cab window above the middle line, albeit a small area, was painted black.

Model constructors should note that throughout the history of these engines in their original condition, there were several small changes in the position of the nameplates to suit revised ideas of lining position, the 'Golden Arrow' side arrow and so on. Since it is not possible to quote all of these changes in this book, photographs should be consulted for determining the actual prototype position.

The lettering and numerals were an

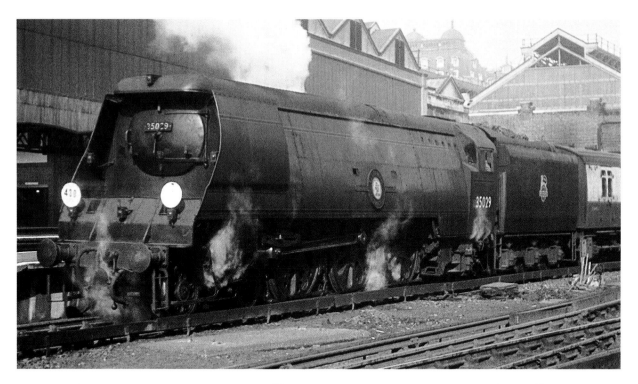

Above:
No 35029 *Ellerman Lines* was repainted in July 1952 with the unfulfilled intention that it would be paired with the newly converted coal weighing tender. Note the cab side lined in a panel: engine and tender lining styles do not match. It is seen here at Victoria Station in 1956. (CR/NRM)

Left:
No 35007 *Aberdeen Commonwealth* at Waterloo in June 1957 shows the normal (for Bulleid Pacifics), but non-standard, lining on BR green. (CR)

interesting hybrid style: the early years of war brought shortages which included green paint and it was realised that economies could be effected if the early Bulleid 'gilt' style of lettering and numerals were to be replaced by yellow (officially 'old gold') with the blocking shot with yellow, to give the effect of highlights. Thus the true 'sunshine' style was born and since most engines were being painted black, the initial orders for the transfers in this style called for the colour for the blocking to be green. These transfers were therefore unsuitable for the few express passenger engines still being repainted green between September 1941 and April 1942 and so the former 'gilt' style continued to be used in these cases. In the case

of Nos 21C3–6, blocking was added in black, by hand painting. Note that these early liveries emphasised the size of the 'C' in the number (and it seems that draughtsmen were also encouraged to mark their drawings in the same way, and even the clerks who kept the Engine Record Cards !).

Nos 21C4 and 5 were completed to the same standard as No 21C3 and entered traffic in malachite green livery with yellow lining. No 21C6 was completed in malachite livery but the completion of No 21C7 coincided with a high-level decision by the SR to cease using green paint for new locomotives and those requiring repainting. So although during construction No 21C7 received malachite green paint but no lining, it was repainted in

black before entering traffic in June 1942. Nos 21C5 and 6 did not retain green livery very long, as they were both repainted into black for their naming ceremonies. Nos 21C8 to 10 were finished in black livery and entered traffic in June-July 1942.

1945-47

All of the second series locomotives were placed in traffic in black livery, but most were soon repainted in malachite green. The matt finish had been found to be difficult to keep clean and so, for the future, the livery was overcoated with gloss varnish. The first engine to be repainted in malachite livery after the 'black' period was deemed to be over, if not completely finished with, was No 21C12, in time for its naming ceremony in April 1945. The lower line on this locomotive was positioned along the cut-out above the driving wheels, but at both the firebox and in front of the cylinders the yellow paint had to be applied over the heads of fasteners. Apart from being more difficult for the liners who applied the paint, these small protrusions trapped dirt and spoiled the finish. Curiously, No 21C11, alone among the second series, was given lining that followed that of the first series by leaving a green strip below the bottom yellow line, above the cut-out. By this time, 'sunshine' transfers with black blocking were available.

SOUTHERN
3578

Above:
Southern 'sunshine' lettering on malachite green.

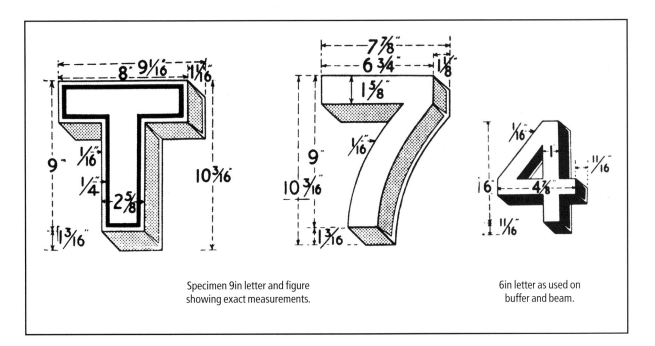

Specimen 9in letter and figure
showing exact measurements.

6in letter as used on
buffer and beam.

Left:
No 21C5 *Canadian Pacific* photographed around March 1948 at Eastleigh. This was the first BR numbering scheme, with 'sunshine' lettering used for the tender inscription. The cowl is black and the wheels are green with black axle ends and tyres. (CR/ST)

Above:
The right hand
side nameplate
of No 21C2
Union Castle. (SLS)

After the war, when Nos 21C1 and 21C2 were repainted in green, they received the repositioned centre line and so conformed to the other engines of the class except that the full complement of cast plates was retained. In other respects the lining followed the 1941 scheme for No 21C3, the lower line being separated from the cut-out by approximately 2in of green.

Note that the screens at the rear of the cab were painted green and the lining was carried around at least as far as the vertical handrail. The beading on the leading edge of the casing and smoke deflectors was generally plain green, the lining not continuing from the casing platework. A band along the top edge of the smoke deflectors approximately 3in wide was painted black. Wheels were green, with tyres and axle ends black, and the cowling was finished in gloss black. The remainder of the roof casing had a matt black appearance.

1948

Locomotives requiring complete repainting in 1948 were given their BR number and, until late in 1948, a 'BRITISH RAILWAYS' inscription on the tender in the then current form of lettering in 'sunshine' style, a modified style

without the highlights, or 10in Gill Sans medium. The tables provide more detail of the actual style of the livery. Unless the works visit was very brief, locomotives were generally renumbered, and if the paint work was sufficiently good so that only worn or damaged areas required attention then it was Eastleigh practice to release the engine back into traffic with 'SOUTHERN' still on the tender, but with a BR number. While malachite green was used, the SR used 'old gold' yellow for lettering and numerals, and as far as possible, attempted to match the styles of the tender lettering with those of the cab-side numerals.

From June 1948 onwards, numberplates were fitted to the smokebox door and the roundels removed. These numberplates were black with white numerals. Note that there could be some difficulty in finding a position for these plates, and there were variations: this was due to the proximity of the circular door boss and the upper lampiron/disc bracket. In some cases, a segment was machined in the base of the numberplate to facilitate location close to the boss.

The early engines of the third series were completed in this period and at an interview with Mr John Miller, Eastleigh Paintshop Foreman, Mr Barry Fletcher obtained the details of the materials used on No 35021 to

provide the malachite green finish. Note that the interior of the cab was yellow ochre colour and that the nameplates and bufferbeam used the same red colour in this interpretation of the then current BR requirements. Note also that the cowling was glossy black and the wheels were green, with tyres and axle ends black.

When attached to Light Pacific tenders, the locomotives were unlined, but as soon as the correct 6,000-gallon tender became available then the yellow lining was applied.

Boiler, Frames etc					
Boiler (No 1098)	Red Oxide	30lb		Filling	47lb
Boiler Clothing	Red Lead	30lb		Lead primer	1 gal.
Frames (Inside and Out)	Roof Lead	22lb		Nulac undercoat green	6 pints
Frames (Outside)	Black Varnish	10lb		Nulac Finishing green	6 pints
	Finishing Coat	4 pints		Nulac HD varnish	6 pints
Ashpan	Black Lacquer	5 pints	**Front of Engine and Smokebox top**		
Firebox Lagging	Roof lead	11½lb	(ie around the chimney)		
	Drop Black	11½lb		Drop Black	
				(a heat resistant paint)	
Wheels			**Cab**		
Derust, clean and paint				Lead Colour, Filling, Stain	
	Lead Colour	10lb		Yellow Ochre	8lb
Rub down etc	Stopping	15lb		Varnish (Dockers)	3 pints
	Filling	16lb	**Name Plates and Plank** (ie Buffer Beam)		
Rub down etc	Undercoat Nulac			Pink Primer	1lb
	(green)	½gal.		Red Lake	2lb
	Nulac finish (green)	5 pints		Stopping	
	Nulac HD Varnish	3 pints		(for the plank)	2lb
Engine			**Brake Gear**		
	Roof Lead colour	21lb		Black Lacquer	

MERCHANT • CHANNEL PACKET • NAVY CLASS

© 2004 Richard Green

MERCHANT • CUNARD WHITE STAR • NAVY CLASS

© 2004 Richard Green

Right:
For the BR blue livery, Eastleigh initially translated the Bulleid scheme into blue with red lining for No 35024 *East Asiatic Company*, February 1949.(CR/ST)

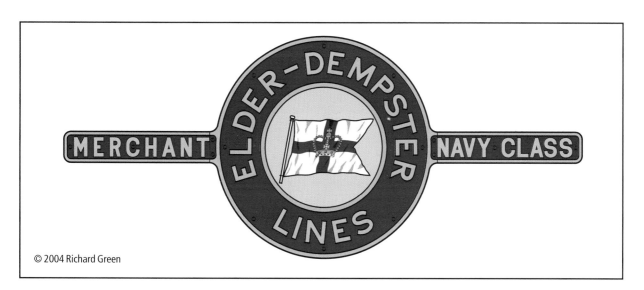

© 2004 Richard Green

© 2004 Richard Green

Left:
At the end of March 1949 the red lines were replaced by black outlined in white. The cylinders and front skirting were finished in black. A month later the wheels were painted black and the black skirting was extended. This became standard for the class as on No 35017 *Belgian Marine*, July 1949. (CR/FNR)

The malachite green scheme continued (although in the spring of 1949, practice changed in that the wheels, cylinders and front splashskirt were painted black) without lettering on the tender until BR decided that the 'Merchant Navy' class was to be painted in express passenger blue livery. In February 1949 No 35024 was repainted in blue and red: the blue replacing the malachite green and the red replacing the yellow for the horizontal lining, with the lower red line touching the cut-out above the driving wheels. The tender received a handpainted BR crest. This livery was not approved and No 35024 was taken back into the Works for the red lines to be removed and the cylinders and casing in front to be painted black. Two lines in black edged in white were applied horizontally over the blue finish.

However, this too, was not approved and next the black of the cylinders and front casing was extended to the lower firebox casing, lower cab sides, and lower tender sides: these black areas became known as the 'splash skirt'. The wheels were painted black. The lower lining was raised slightly above the position of the former red line, leaving a strip of blue below. This scheme was approved and became standard for the class commencing in July 1949, although Nos 35011, 35014 and 35023 did not require repainting while this scheme was current and so did not appear in blue. Although the blue has been described as 'dark', it was, in fact, not as dark as the BR experimental blue of 1948. The cab-side number was painted in 'straw' colour using 10in Gill Sans numerals.

Note that the lower of the two lines was raised sufficiently so that it was clear of the heads of the fasteners that had earlier protruded on to the yellow (or red) line. This was because the finer white/black/white lining suffered greater interference from the protrusions and caused an unacceptable result.

It is interesting to note that the Bulleid Pacifics were given special dispensation not to have smoke deflectors painted black.

At this time nameplates continued to be painted with a red ground. The screens at the rear of the cab were painted blue without lining, except on the few first series engines remaining without modified cabs when the lower line was carried around the curve, as it also was on the

curved edge on the tender side of the cab entrance.

Nos 21C1 and 2 when repainted into blue, the cast plates being removed.

1951-REBUILDING

Although many felt that the blue livery suited the 'Merchant Navy' class, not unexpectedly, as a colour it was not stable. The livery was expected to last about five years under the BR maintenance system, but great difficulty was found when 'touching-up' was needed after a couple of years of service as the existing shades of blue on the locomotive could vary considerably from new paint. As with other BR liveries at this time, the Eastleigh Paintshop foreman found that it was also more costly to apply, apart from the facts that it did not endure as well or appear as attractive as the bright, malachite green. A decision was therefore taken to cease the use of blue and to use the BR standard green shade with black and orange lining. Also, with this decision came the requirement to paint the ground of nameplates in black.

At this time, the Bulleid Pacifics had an outline unique among British locomotives and when the experimental apple green liveries were applied to the Light Pacifics in 1948 it was found

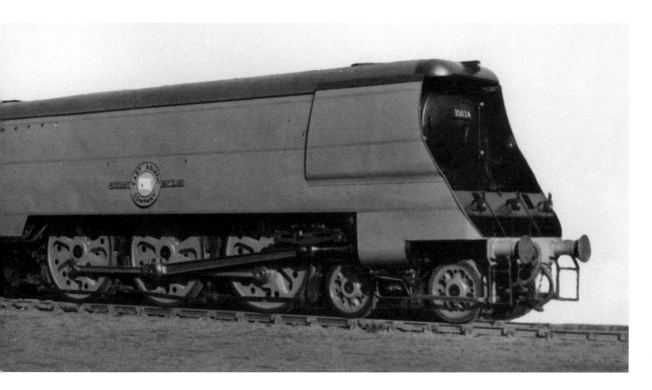

that the lining appeared very weak. When the BR green scheme was introduced in 1949 on the smaller Pacifics, the lining was strengthened: this was applied as two horizontal lines but the black line was made wider than the BR standard and the orange lines abutted the black, rather than being separated with the ground colour green showing between. In June 1951, No 35024 was repainted in this style, having been the first to receive blue livery and the first to lose it. The black splash skirting was retained as before, with the larger sized BR crest.

When the 'guinea-pig' locomotives (Nos 35012/13/21 in 1952 and No 35020 in July 1953) with experimental cut-down tenders were painted, the coal bunker became green and the horizontal lining no longer suited the tender and so this was now painted with the lining in a panel and with the orange lines separated from the black by the green background as was BR standard practice, ie 'spaced out'. The black splash skirt was eliminated and the smaller-sized BR crest was applied in the centre of the lined panel. To attempt to match the style of the tender, the cab sides were now lined in a panel without the black splash skirt, and the horizontal lines on the casing extended only as far as a vertical joint line, at the front of the lower cab sides (ie, not exactly back to the front window frame). The front casing (where this was retained on No 35021)

and the lower firebox casing were still painted black in the style of the 'splash skirt' and the lining was 'spaced out'.

The self-weighing tender, No 3343, was also painted in this style, and while it was working with No 35014 the engine required repainting (November 1953) and was finished in the revised style with spaced out lining. In July 1952, No 35029 was prepared to work with this tender and was also finished in the revised lining style, but in the event, No 35029 ran with a conventionally painted tender with large crest.

The removal of the casing ahead of the cylinders was aesthetically disastrous, especially for the first series where a severe discontinuity of line was caused when compared with the cut-out above the driving wheels. To mitigate this, it became practice to raise the top of the black splash skirting so that a clean line of demarcation was obtained right along the length of the engine. Thus a band of black about 2in wide now appeared above the cut-out and the orange/black/orange lining was commensurately raised to suit.

When it was decided to cut down all Bulleid Pacific tenders in 1956, it was decided to continue the lining as a panel, 'spaced out' in style, and without the black splash skirt. For the engines, it was decided to restore the black splash

Above:
A works photograph of No 35024 *East Asiatic Company* with nameplate uncovered. This colour scheme was shortlived, being replaced by blue with white-outlined black lining.

Right:
No 35020 *Bibby Line* in 1951 shows that the blue was not a stable colour when a part of the casing needed to be repainted. (CR/PCS)

Southern Smokebox plates

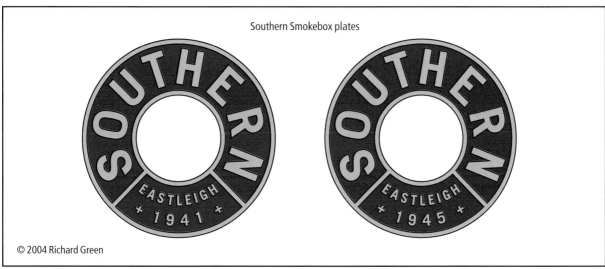

Above:
No 35007 *Aberdeen Commonwealth* at Exeter Central in 1948 whilst working the 'Devon Belle'. The locomotive is in Southern livery but has been renumbered using 'sunshine' style numerals on the cab side. Note the tender ladder with two rungs and the original form of the cab with rain strip added. (MP 92^1/$_2$)

skirt to the cab but this would be lined in a now smaller panel, 'spaced out' in style, but the unspaced 'bold' style would be restored for the horizontal lines on the side casings. The following are believed to have received this style: Nos 35001 (6/56); 35007 (9/56); 35021 (2/57); and 35011 (8/57), the latter receiving the large second style BR emblem with right-facing lion on the right-hand side of the tender.

During 1958, the presence of the BR water treatment system on a locomotive became denoted by a pale yellow circle, 3in in diameter, painted on the cab-side below the number. At around the same time, the BR power classification '8P' was painted in 2in straw Gill Sans characters above the cab-side number. Later, the circle was replaced by a triangle.

Tender No 3345, not cut down, was painted with a black band along the raves for purposes of road trials with locomotive No 35020 in May 1956. In July 1956, this tender was transferred to No 35028 without repainting and it ran thus until September 1958, when the tender was repainted and given the new-style BR emblem. Thus, No 35028, ultimately the last 'Merchant Navy' to be rebuilt and still with the original horizontal lining on engine and tender, received the second style of BR emblem in the large size, with right-facing lion, on the tender.

THE REBUILT LOCOMOTIVES

The standard BR green locomotive livery scheme was used with 'spaced out' black and orange lining. The running plate valance was lined in orange only, as if an elongated panel.

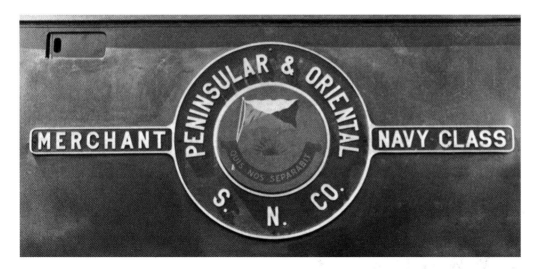

No 35020 was the locomotive chosen for road trials from May to July 1956 and for the purpose was coupled to an unmodified tender (No 3345). The tender was painted as though the tender had been cut down, but uniquely, a wide black band was painted along the raves.

No 35030 in April 1958 may have been the first 'Merchant Navy' to receive the yellow symbol denoting BR water treatment. However, it was claimed that such a circle caused confusion with Western Region route restriction codes and the water treatment circle was replaced by a yellow triangle! This was an equilateral triangle (ie the three sides had equal lengths), which stood 4in high, the position being the same as for the circle (there were occasions where the circle could be made out underneath the triangle). No 35028 was the first noted with the yellow triangle after a works visit to Eastleigh, week ending 29/7/61.

In May 1962, No 35012 was repainted and this included a red ground to the nameplates. Future nameplate repaints were in this colour and it appears that the shade was the same as that used for the buffer beams.

Since the 'Merchant Navy' class was not expected to work off the Southern Region, it was not included in the list of classes to receive Electrification Warning Signs (EWS) in 1960. However, some locomotives later did receive EWS as a result of working railtours over 'foreign' lines (No 35026 in 1966) or when allocated to Weymouth shed (Nos 35008/ 35014/35028/35030 on rear of tender only) where practice was made of applying the signs to this class.

Above: An atmospheric view of No 35026 *Ellerman Lines* at Southampton Central, February 1966. (CR/LFF)

Tables of Dates of Significant Alterations to 'Merchant Navy' Class Locomotives

General Note: The use of italics in the tables indicates that the precise date is not known; c. indicates circa, about or around; p. indicates 'possibly'; 'yes' and 'not' mean respectively that the modification did or did not take place; A '?' mark indicates that it is not known whether the modification took place or not; A '-' mark means that the modification did not take place.

First Series (a)

Event or Modification	21C1/35001 Channel Packet	21C2/35002 Union Castle
Completed[1]	2/41	6/41
To Traffic	5/6/41	16/6/41
Early alterations[2]	by 8/41	footnote 2
Named	10/3/41	4/7/41
Inverted Horseshoe to Roundel[3]	c.1/42	c.1/42
Repainted Wartime Black	12/43	3/6/44
Hood/Flared Deflectors	26/8/43	3/6/44
Repainted Malachite	3/12/45	22/6/46
Standard Deflectors	c. 8/47	c. 5/47[4]
Renumbered[5]	21/10/49	4/1/50
Repainted BR Blue	21/10/49	4/1/50
Cab Modified	6/11/50	2/1/54
Sliding Covers (Whistle & Manifold valves)	p. 5/52	22/8/52
Repainted BR Green	17/5/52	3/7/51
Front Casing removed	p.10/53	22/8/52
Safety Valves resited	16/6/56	27/8/55
Modified Crank Pin (before rebuilding)[6]	p. 6/56	yes
Plain Coupling Rods (before rebuilding)	p. 6/56	yes
2nd BR Emblem (tender)	15/8/59	17/5/58
Locomotive Rebuilt	15/8/59	17/5/58
AWS	15/8/59	9/4/60
Speedometer	21/1/61	9/4/60
Outside Piston Valve Spindle Pockets[7]	15/8/59	p.11/62
Locomotive Withdrawn	11/64	2/64

Tenders:

21C1/35001:	3111 (2/41),	3112 (5/41),	3111 (5/41),	3349 (3/65).
21C2/35002:	3112 (6/41),	3115 (3/52),	3112 (3/52).	

[1] 21C1 was completed in matt malachite green with yellow lines. 21C2 ran its initial trials without the lines having been applied, but these were added before naming.

[2] The early alterations on 21C1 included: moving the numberplate from the front angle to the lower, vertical position; raising the three lower lamps/disc brackets; provision of footholds on the front angle; provision of footsteps below the RHS front buffer with footblock on the buffer stock (previously only the LHS buffer was so equipped); enlargement of the slot in the top casing in front of the chimney to a much larger air passageway around the chimney. These alterations were incorporated into 21C2 during construction. Also, 21C2 was not provided with a chimney cover and the hole in the top casing where the whistle was sited was enlarged and became a 'slot'. Later the whistle was moved up to the centreline of the locomotive.

[3] When built, 21C1 and 21C2 both had a 'SOUTHERN' ownership plate in the form of an inverted horseshoe mounted on the smokebox door. These were replaced by roundels which added the place of construction and the year date to the ownership inscription. Bradley gives 2/42 for 21C1 and 12/41 for 21C2, while Fry indicates early 1942 for 21C1 and 2/42 for 21C2.

[4] 21C2 seems to have received standard length deflectors 'on shed', initially without lining and without 'Devon Belle' battens.

[5] Both 21C1 and 21C2 retained their cast number and 'SOUTHERN' ownership plates until renumbered when these two locomotives were repainted in BR express passenger blue with straw coloured Gill Sans numerals and the first BR crest in the large size.

[6] There were two types of modified retaining caps on the crank pins. First came a washer, nut and taper pin; later, four studs and nuts retained a circular cap and this arrangement also proved satisfactory for the return crank of the Walschaerts gear when the locos were rebuilt.

[7] No 35001 was fitted with the smaller 'inside' type of pocket when it was rebuilt. No 35002 was rebuilt without pockets, but both locomotives were later fitted with the larger 'inside and outside' type.

First Series (b)

Event or Modification	21C3/ 35003 Royal Mail	21C4 35004 Cunard White Star	21C5/ 35005 Canadian Pacific	21C6/ 35006 Peninsular & Oriental S. N. Co	21C7/ 35007 Aberdeen Commonwealth	21C8/ 35008 Orient Line	21C9/ 35009 Shaw Savill	21C10/ 35010 Blue Star
To Traffic	13/9/41	12/41	13/1/42	14/1/42	6/42	6/42	25/6/42	31/7/42
Wartime Black Livery[8]	5/43	7/43	3/42	5/42	6/42	6/42	6/42	7/42
Named	24/10/41	1/1/42	27/3/42	4/6/42	30/7/42	2/11/42	30/7/42	18/12/42
Hood/Flared Deflectors[9]	9/44	1/44	18/3/44	27/4/44	17/8/44	1/43[10]	6/43	3/43
Repainted Malachite	3/11/45	4/5/46	2/2/46	29/9/46	26/7/47	30/8/47	11/46	6/6/47
Standard Deflectors	22/5/47	10/10/46	c. 6/47	c.7/47	by 5/47	c. 5/47[11]	p.11/46	3/47
Renumbered[12]	7/6/48	19/4/48	18/3/48[13]	11/12/48	25/12/48	20/7/49	31/8/49	13/12/48
Repainted BR Blue	16/6/50	12/7/49	17/2/50	21/3/51	31/3/50	20/7/49	31/8/49	25/11/49
Cab Modified	16/6/50	1/11/50	17/2/50	21/3/51	31/3/50	30/8/47[14]	1/3/53	25/11/49
Sliding Covers[15]	26/4/52	p.2/53	p. 7/52	1952-3	p.12/52	p.5/52	p.3/53	21/11/52
Repainted BR Green	9/8/53	14/2/53	13/2/54	7/9/53	20/12/52	21/5/52	1/3/53	21/11/52
Front Casing removed	p.8/53	p.2/53	p.7/52	9/53	12/52	p.10/53	p.3/53	21/11/52
Safety Valves resited	27/3/55	5/11/55	13/2/54	9/7/55	26/6/55	18/10/53	?	-
Modified Crank Pin[16]	27/3/55	?	yes	yes	by 3/55	p. not	-	by 8/55
Plain Coupling Rods[17]	by 1/56	by 3/56	23/12/54	5/56	9/56	5/56	1/56	-
Locomotive Rebuilt	5/9/59	12/7/58	6/6/59	17/10/59	21/6/58	1/6/57	23/3/57	12/1/57
2nd BR Emblem (tender)	5/9/59	12/7/58	6/6/59	17/10/59	21/6/58	1/6/57	23/3/57	9/12/61
AWS	5/9/59	28/9/59	17/12/60	17/10/59	10/10/59	7/5/60	5/11/60	30/8/59
PV Spindle Pockets (o/s)[18]	5/9/59	29/9/62	6/6/59	17/10/59	p. 10/62	p. 4/60	p.12/62	aft.7/62
Speedometer	7/10/61	20/2/60	17/12/60[13]	21/1/61	15/4/61	7/5/60	13/2/60	9/12/61
Locomotive Withdrawn	9/7/67	10/65	10/65	8/64	7/67	7/67	9/64	9/66

Note: Grab handle fitted on smokebox door before rebuilding: 35004, 35005, 35006, 35008.

Tenders:

21C3/35003:	3113 (9/41),	3117 (2/44).	
21C4/35004:	3114 (10/41),	3113 (1/44),	3121 (10/65).
21C5/35005:	3115 (12/41),	3348 (8/65).	
21C6/35006:	3116 (12/41) throughout.		
21C7/35007:	3117 (6/42),	3114 (5/44),	3127 (9/66).
21C8/35008:	3118 (6/42),	3343 (2/62),	3118 (10/64).
21C9/35009:	3119 (6/42) throughout.		
21C10/35010:	3120 (7/42),	3122 (12/64).	

[8] Nos 21C3-7 were painted in malachite green when built but Nos 21C8-10 were black when built.

[9] Nos 21C10 was involved from 12/42 in smoke clearance trials. Nos 21C6 and 7 were also involved.

[10] Bradley, Fry and Derry give 6/43, 1/43 and 3/43 respectively for the fitting of a hood to 21C8: it is possible that there were a number of variations, but details or photographs have not come to light.

[11] Probably fitted 'on shed' whilst the locomotive was still in wartime black livery.

[12] The following livery styles occurred on renumbering:
Malachite green with yellow lines, 'Sunshine' style numerals and BR lettering: 35003/4/5;
Malachite green with yellow lines, BR Gill Sans lettering and numerals: 35006;
Malachite green with yellow lines, SR style numerals but retaining 'SOUTHERN' lettering: 35007/10;
BR express passenger blue, Gill Sans numerals and first BR crest in the large size: 35008/9.

[13] Renumbered 18/3/48, initially with s-prefix as s21C5 when a Berkley Mechanical Stoker and Flaman Speed Recorder were fitted. Renumbered 35005 (ex-works 8/4/48) after adjustments to the mechanical stoker. The mechanical stoker was removed in April 1951.

[14] In August 1947, 21C8 was the first MN to receive a 'Vee' fronted cab, to improve forward visibility and make cleaning by the crew easier. The two side windows were retained until June 1949 when the three-window pattern which became standard, was fitted.

[15] These covers refer to the whistle and manifold valves.

[16] Before rebuilding there were two types of modified retaining caps on the crank pins. First came a washer nut and taper pin; later, four studs and nuts retained a circular cap and this arrangement also proved satisfactory for the return crank of the Walschaerts gear and was adopted when the locomotives were rebuilt.

[17] Before rebuilding.

[18] No 35005 received 'step' type covers over the holes in the angled running plate and Nos 35003/6/8 had the small 'inside' pockets. These locos and 35004/7-10 later received the larger 'inside and outside' type.

Second Series (a)

NB. All of the second series were constructed with 'short' smoke deflectors. Nos 21C11-15 were built without grab handles on the smokebox door, but all received them shortly after.

Event or Modification	21C11/ 35011 *General Steam Navigation*	21C12/ 35012 *United States Line*	21C13/ 35013 *Blue Funnel*	21C14/ 35014 *Nederland Line*	21C15/ 35015 *Rotterdam Lloyd*
To Traffic (Wartime Black)	30/12/44	13/1/45	2/45	13/2/45	5/3/45
Named	20/2/45	10/4/45	17/4/45	27/11/45	27/11/45
Repainted Malachite	1/47	6/4/45	11/46	24/11/45	24/11/45
Standard Deflectors	*p.1/47*	3/47	11/46	*c. 1/47*	*p.2/47*
Renumbered[19]	6/11/48	17/3/49	10/8/48[20]	3/5/49	8/6/49
Repainted BR Blue	-	17/2/51	5/8/50	-	7/2/51
Cab Modified	29/9/50	17/3/49	13/12/52	3/5/49	8/6/49
Sliding Covers (Whistle & Manifold valves)	*p. 4/53*	5/7/52	p.12/52	by11/53	p. 4/52
Repainted BR Green	18/11/51	5/7/52	13/12/52	25/8/51	7/6/53
Front Casing removed	*p.4/53*[21]	5/7/52	p.12/52	p.11/52	p.1953
Safety Valves resited	?	?	?	3/7/54	24/4/54
Modified Crank Pin (before rebuilding)[22]	-	-	-	-	c. 1954
Plain Coupling Rods (before rebuilding)	3/56	c. 1956	-	-	p.6/56
Locomotive Rebuilt	11/7/59	2/3/57	26/5/56	7/7/56	21/6/58
2nd BR Emblem (tender)	11/7/59	12/5/62	3/6/61	7/4/62	21/6/58
AWS	3/6/61	14/11/59	28/11/59	29/10/59	14/11/59
Outside PV Spindle Pockets[23]	11/7/59	*p.9/60*	*p.11/62*	*by 4/62*	*p. 6/62*
Speedometer	3/6/61	17/9/60	3/6/61	23/12/60	25/6/60
Locomotive Withdrawn	2/66	4/67	7/67	3/67	2/64

Tenders:

21C11/35011: 3121 (12/44), 3129 (10/65).
21C12/35012: 3122 (1/45), 3343 (7/52), 3122 (7/52), 3120 (12/64).
21C13/35013: 3123 (2/45), 3124 (8/50).
21C14/35014: 3124 (2/45), 3123 (6/50), 3343 (10/52), 3126 (7/56), 3345 (3/65), 3115 (8/65).
21C15/35015: 3126 (3/45), 3343 (7/56), 3123 (6/58).

[19] The following livery styles occurred on renumbering:
Malachite green with yellow lines, BR Gill Sans numerals but without tender lettering: 35012/14/15. No 35013 was repainted thus on 5/2/49 after initial renumbering in 8/48;
Malachite green with yellow lines, BR Gill Sans lettering and numerals: 35011;
Malachite green with yellow lines, SR style numerals but retaining 'SOUTHERN' lettering: 35013;
[20] 35013 was repainted on 5/2/49, see footnote 19, above.
[21] 21C11 was unique in being built with a bulbous casing between the buffer beam and cylinders. The bulbous lower part of this casing was removed about the time of renumbering in 11/48. The section remaining appeared as other locos of the second series and was probably removed in 4/53.

[22] Before rebuilding, there were two types of modified retaining caps on the crank pins. First came a washer nut and taper pin; later, four studs and nuts retained a circular cap and this arrangement also proved satisfactory for the return crank of the Walschaerts gear and was adopted when the locomotives were rebuilt.
[23] No 35011 was rebuilt with the small 'inside' type pocket and No 35014 was fitted with this type after rebuilding, possibly 10/59. Later, all of 35011-15 received the larger 'inside and outside' type.

Second Series (b)

NB. Nos 21C16-20 had a grab handle fitted to the smokebox door during construction.

Event or Modification	21C16/ 35016 Elders Fyffes	21C17/ 35017 Belgian Marine	21C18/ 35018 British India Line	21C19/ 35019[24] French Line C. G. T.	21C20/ 35020 Bibby Line
To Traffic (Wartime Black)	14/3/45	17/4/45	7/5/45	7/6/45	30/6/45
Named	5/7/45	22/10/45	13/12/45	22/9/45	18/10/45
Repainted Malachite	17/1/47	21/10/45	18/8/45	20/9/45	12/8/45
Standard Deflectors	*p. 1/47*	*p. 3/47*	*by 7/10/46[25]*	*by 8/47*	7/47
Renumbered[26]	23/10/48	24/4/48[27]	29/5/48	11/5/48[28]	11/5/48[29]
Repainted BR Blue	31/5/50	11/7/49	27/9/49	13/1/50	2/6/50
Cab Modified	24/6/49	24/4/48	5/48	11/5/48	11/5/48
Sliding Covers (Whistle & Manifold valves)	*p. 3/53*	*p.4/53*	*p. 5/53*	*by 7/53*	20/6/52
Repainted BR Green	15/3/53	1/4/53	3/7/51	7/6/53	20/6/52
Front Casing removed	c.1953	c.1953	12/7/52	by 7/53	20/6/52
Safety Valves resited	29/8/54	4/8/54	?	14/10/55	3/7/53[30]
Modified Crank Pin (before rebuilding)[31]	yes	yes	-	*by 10/54[32]*	-
Plain Coupling Rods (before rebuilding)	9/56	12/55	-	by 3/56	-
Locomotive Withdrawn Rebuilt	20/4/57	6/4/57	11/2/56	16/5/59	30/4/56
2nd BR Emblem (tender)	20/4/57	6/4/57	9/5/59	16/5/59	13/5/61
AWS	21/11/59	31/10/59	17/12/60	17/10/59	1/8/59
PV Spindle Pockets[33]	*p. 8/62*	*p. 5/62*	*p. 1/62*	16/5/59	*p. 4/63*
Speedometer	25/3/61	15/4/61	20/2/60	25/2/61	13/5/61
Locomotive Withdrawn	8/65	7/66	8/64	9/65	2/65

Tenders:

21C16/35016:	3125 (3/45) throughout.					
21C17/35017:	3127 (4/45),	10123 (LMS, 4/48),	3127 (6/48),	3114 (9/66).		
21C18/35018:	3129 (5/45),	3343 (7/52),	3346 (10/52),	3118 (12/61),	3343 (10/64).	
21C19/35019:	3128 (12/41),	10219 (LMS, 4/48),	3128 (5/48).			
21C20/35020:	3130 (6/42),	10373 (LMS, 5/48),	3130 (6/48),	3347 (6/52),	3345 (5/56),	3344 (7/56).

[24] No 35019 was fitted with a single chimney and blastpipe during its 1951 General overhaul, returning to service 22/6/51. This chimney was removed and replaced by the Bulleid multiple jet design in March 1956.

[25] Earlier (by 6/46), No 35018 had received a rearwards extension of about 12in to its original deflectors.

[26] The following livery styles occurred on renumbering:

Malachite green with yellow lines, numerals and lettering in 'Sunshine' style: 35018;

Malachite green with yellow lines, BR Gill Sans lettering on 35016, but the cabside numerals were an oddity: when renumbered (10/48) Gill Sans numerals were applied but when the modified cab was fitted (6/49) Southern Style numerals were used.

Malachite green with yellow lines, SR style numerals, retaining 'SOUTHERN' lettering: 35017, 35019/20.

[27] 21C17, renumbered 35017, participated in the 1948 Locomotive Exchange trials and ran temporarily with a black painted ex-LMS tender for the purpose (fitted w/e 24/4/48). Locomotive had a Flaman recorder fitted for the same reason. On return to normal service, 15/6/48, its own tender was refitted still in its former SR livery.

[28] 21C19, renumbered 35019, participated in the 1948 Locomotive Exchange trials and ran temporarily with a black painted ex-LMS tender for the purpose (fitted 13/4/48). Locomotive had a Flaman recorder fitted for the same reason. On return to normal service, 29/5/48, its own tender 3128 was refitted still in its former SR livery. On

18/5/49, 35019 was repainted with a 'blank' tender.

[29] 21C20, renumbered 35020, was prepared for but did not take part in the 1948 Locomotive Exchange trials: it was given extra long smoke deflectors and temporarily paired with a black painted ex-LMS tender for the purpose. The locomotive had a Flaman recorder fitted for the same reason. On return to normal service, 3/6/48, its own tender was refitted still in its former SR livery. The extra long smoke deflectors were retained until rebuilding.

[30] 35020 was fitted at this date with new cylinder drain valves, having two drain pipes per cylinder (three previously).

[31] Before rebuilding, there were two types of modified retaining caps on the crank pins. First came a washer nut and taper pin; later, four studs and nuts retained a circular cap and this arrangement also proved satisfactory for the return crank of the Walschaerts Gear and was adopted when the locomotives were rebuilt.

[32] No 35019 reverted to the Curl type crank pin by 9/56.

[33] No 35019 was rebuilt with a hole in the angled running plate to accommodate the piston valve spindle, covered by a step with a deep valance for protection. Nos 35016-18/20 had been rebuilt without pockets, but No 35018 was later fitted with the smaller 'inside' type pocket. Subsequently, Nos 35016-17/19-20 were fitted with the larger 'inside and outside' type of pocket, but No 35018 retained the smaller type until withdrawal.

Third Series (a)

NB. All of the third series were constructed with standard length smoke deflectors and 'Vee' fronted cabs. The trailing truck was fabricated, whereas the first 20 locomotives had cast trucks.

Event or Modification	35021 New Zealand Line	35022 Holland America Line	35023 Holland-Africa Line	35024 East Asiatic Company	35025 Brocklebank Line
To Traffic[34]	11/9/48	9/10/48	6/11/48	13/11/48	27/11/48
Named	24/11/48	24/1/49	24/1/49	5/5/49	20/9/49
Repainted BR Blue	22/11/50	1/7/50	-	29/3/49	17/9/49
Sliding Covers (Whistle & Manifold valves)	26/2/52	c.1952-3	22/3/52	c.1952-3	29/3/52
Repainted BR Green	26/2/52[35]	5/2/52	22/3/52	15/6/51	7/6/52
Front Casing removed	c.8/53	p.3-5/53	p. 5/53	p. 10/52	p. 10/53
Safety Valves resited	10/10/54	-	17/10/54	?	-
Modified Crank Pin (before rebuilding)[36]	2/54	-	10/54	c.8/54	p. 2/55
Plain Coupling Rods (before rebuilding)	2/56	-	12/55	3/56	1/56
Locomotive Rebuilt	20/6/59	19/6/56	16/2/57	2/5/59	15/12/56
2nd BR Emblem (tender)	20/6/59	18/1/58	24/11/62	2/5/59	10/3/62
AWS	6/5/61	17/10/59	15/10/60	24/10/59	7/11/59
Outside PV Spindle Pockets[37]	20/6/59	1/58	11/62	2/5/59	by 6/62
Speedometer	6/5/61	5/11/60	15/10/60	10/12/60	9/7/60
Locomotive Withdrawn	8/65	5/66	7/67	1/65	9/64

Tenders:

35021:	3333 (9/48);	3342 (11/48);	3126 (10/65).		
35022:	3335 (10/48);	3345 (1/49);	3347 (6/56).		
35023:	3341 (11/48) throughout.				
35024:	3333 (11/48);	3346 (2/49);	3123 (11/52);	3343 (5/58);	3346 (12/61).
35025:	3343 (11/48);	3350 (6/52).			

[34] Because of delays in the completion of their 6,000-gallon tenders, Nos 35021, 35022 and 35024 entered traffic coupled to Light Pacific tenders. Owing to the different lining positions on these two classes, this temporary arrangement resulted in both the engine and tender receiving an unlined malachite green livery. When 6,000-gallon tenders became available for attaching to the engines, the yellow lining was added with No 35021's tender receiving Gill Sans lettering (11/48) and No 35022's having no lettering applied (1/49). No 35024 was completely repainted into a trial version of BR Blue with red lining (2/49) but this was quickly followed by a number of minor variations to the livery before the standard with black and white lining was decided (3/49). Nos 35023/5 entered service in the current version of full malachite green livery.
[35] Ex-works with its tender cut down and other 'guinea pig' alterations.

[36] Before rebuilding, there were two types of modified retaining caps on the crank pins. First came a washer nut and taper pin; later, four studs and nuts retained a circular cap and this arrangement also proved satisfactory for the return crank of the Walschaerts gear and was adopted when the locomotives were rebuilt.
[37] 35022 was the first to receive the extended outside piston valve spindles in January 1958 and received 'thimble' type pockets covering the holes in the angled running plate. No 35024 received the 'step' type covers over the holes in the angled running plate. No 35021 was the first locomotive to be rebuilt with the smaller 'inside' type pockets. No 35025 received the 'inside' type after rebuilding (by 6/62). Later, all of Nos 35021-25 received the larger 'inside and outside' type of pocket, No 35022 by 8/62, 35024 in 7/63.

Third Series (b)

NB. All of the third series were constructed with standard length smoke deflectors and 'Vee' fronted cabs. The trailing truck was fabricated, whereas the first 20 locomotives had cast trucks.

Event or Modification	35026 Lamport & Holt Line	35027 Port Line	35028 Clan Line	35029 Ellerman Lines	35030 Elder-Dempster Lines
To Traffic[38]	4/12/48	11/12/48	24/12/48	19/2/49	16/4/49
Named	15/1/51	24/4/50	15/1/51	1/3/51	5/6/50
Repainted BR Blue	8/7/49	21/4/50	13/1/51	26/2/51	1/6/50
Sliding Covers (Whistle & Manifold valves)	14/6/52	22/11/53	12/6/53	c.1952-3	16/5/53
Repainted BR Green	14/6/52	22/11/53	12/6/53	4/7/52	16/5/53
Front Casing removed	p.6/52	22/11/53	12/6/53	4/7/52	c. 5/53
Safety Valves resited	1/55	?	3/12/54	12/12/54	p. not
Modified Crank Pin (before rebuilding)[39]	not	not	by 6/58	by 10/55	by 4/55
Plain Coupling Rods (before rebuilding)	p. 6/56	4/56	7/56	by 8/56[40]	not
Locomotive Rebuilt	26/1/57	12/5/57	7/11/59	26/9/59	26/4/58
2nd BR Emblem (tender)	3/11/62	12/5/57	7/11/59	26/9/59	26/4/58
AWS	28/11/59	28/5/60	7/11/59	26/9/59	11/6/60
Outside PV Spindle Pockets[41]	p.10/62	by10/63	7/11/59	26/9/59	p. 5/62
Speedometer	5/11/60	28/5/60	12/8/61	24/6/61	11/6/60
Locomotive Withdrawn	3/67	9/66	7/67	9/66	7/67

Tenders:

35026:	3260 (12/48);	3350 (7/49);	3130 (6/52);	3349 (3/65);	3111 (4/65).
35027:	3288 (12/48);	3349 (4/49);	3130 (3/65)		
35028:	3344 (12/48);	3345 (7/56);	3126 (3/65);	3342 (10/65).	
35029:	3347 (2/49);	3129 (7/52);	3113 (10/65).		
35030:	3348 (4/49);	3345 (8/65).			

[38] Because of delays in the completion of their 6,000-gallon tenders, Nos 35026, 35027 entered traffic coupled to Light Pacific tenders. Owing to the different lining positions on these two classes, this temporary arrangement resulted in both the engine and tender receiving an unlined malachite green livery. When 6,000-gallon tenders became available for attaching to the engines, No 35026 was repainted in blue. No 35027 had the yellow lining added but the tender had no lettering applied. Nos 35028, 35029 and 35030 came out with full malachite green livery but their tenders were unlettered.
No 35027/30 had front skirting and cylinders painted black.
[39] Before rebuilding, there were two types of modified retaining caps on the crank pins. First came a washer nut and taper pin; later, four studs and nuts retained a circular cap and this arrangement also proved satisfactory for the return crank of the Walschaerts gear and was adopted when the locomotives were rebuilt.

[40] No 35029 appears to have plain front right-hand coupling rod in 10/55; No 35028 had a plain rod on the left-hand side.
[41] Nos 35026, 35027 and 35030 were rebuilt without pockets, but received the larger 'inside and outside' type later. Nos 35028 and 35029 were rebuilt with the smaller 'inside' type but later received the larger 'inside and outside' type of pocket.

Line drawings of the 'Merchant Navy' Class Locomotives

General Note

The casings of the Bulleid Pacifics were constructed using panels of steel sheet or 'Limpet' board fastened to a steel framework. The drawings show only those main sections of panelling, joints and the larger fasteners that were designed to be dismantled during maintenance of the engine. These show clearly in photographs. Sub-sections of panelling, their joints and smaller fasteners were initially finished so as to be almost invisible and for reasons of clarity these are not shown on the drawings. It should be noted that in carrying out certain repairs, sub-sections of panelling could be dismantled and the affected join lines and fasteners thereafter become more obvious.

It is believed that from about 1952, boiler roof casings were generally altered around the safety valves to provide a more open situation, resulting in a recess or 'well'.
This alteration is shown on the drawing.

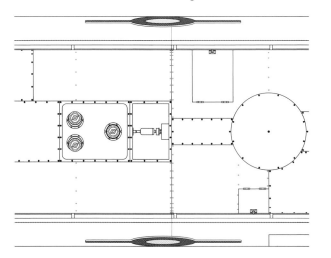

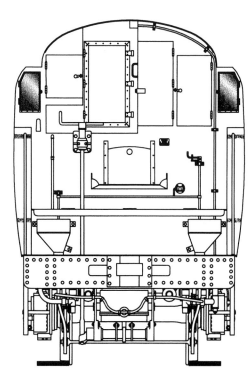

Layout of lockers etc. of a 5,100-gallon high sided tender. The layout for the other tenders is similar.

Scale: 7mm : 1ft

103

Front end of 21C1 *Channel Packet* in the condition it hauled the inaugural postwar 'Golden Arrow' in April 1946. The smoke deflectors were 'flared out' from the original front edge of the casing and differ markedly from the second series and later smoke deflectors in respect of the position with respect to the cowl. The drawing also shows
the earlier form of casing around

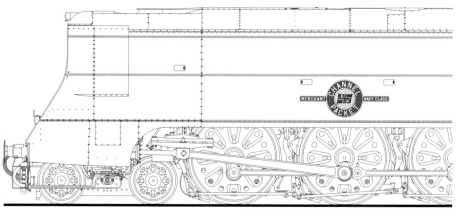

Scale 4mm : 1ft

First series front end fitted with the larger smoke deflectors and the casing panel in front of the cylinders removed. The projection of the front casing used on this series locomotives can be seen. This resulted in the smoke deflector being further forward on the first series compared with the second and third series.

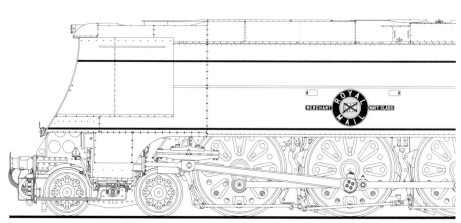

Below is the right-hand (fireman's) side with the injectors and damper levers. Note the spring cover fitted to the cast type of trailing truck and the difference from the fabricated type shown on No 35023.

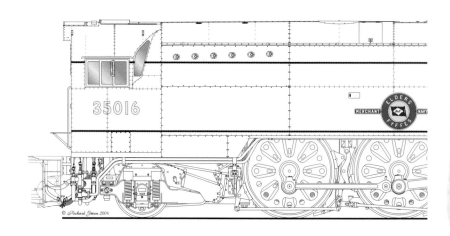

© Richard Green 2004

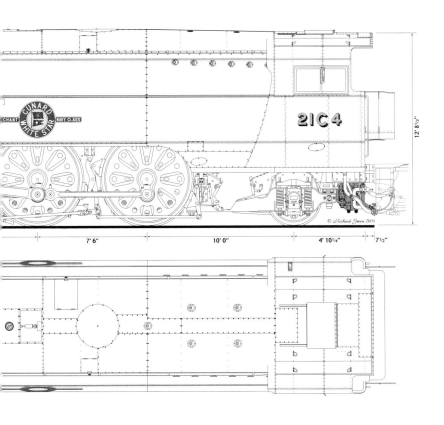

21C4

CUNARD WHITE STAR
CHANT NAVY CLASS

12' 8½"

7' 6"   10' 0"   4' 10¼"   7½"

© Richard Green 2004

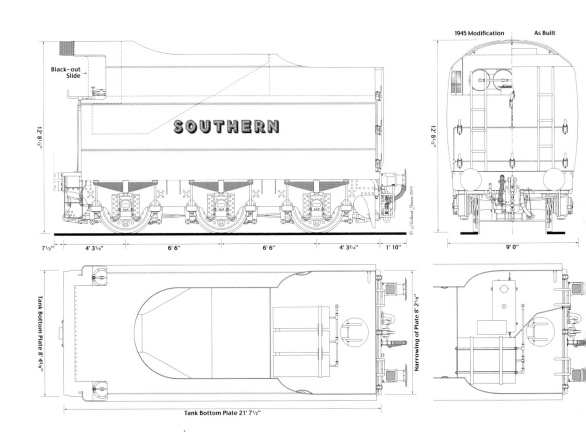

Black-out
Slide

SOUTHERN

12' 8½"

7½"   4' 3¼"   6' 6"   6' 6"   4' 3¾"   1' 10"

© Richard Green 2004

1945 Modification   As Built

12' 8½"

9' 0"

Tank Bottom Plate 8' 4⅜"

Tank Bottom Plate 21' 7½"

Narrowing of Plate 8' 2⅛"

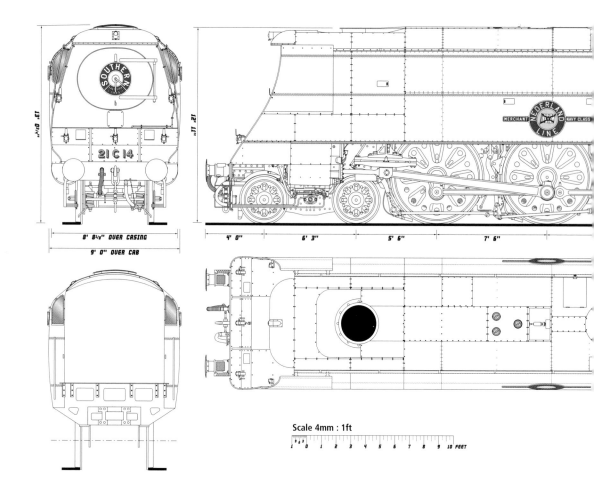

Scale 4mm : 1ft

econd Series – 21C14 *Nederland Line*

own as in November 1945 after repainting in full
uthern post-war malachite livery.

is series incorporated all the modifications made so
 to the first series together with an altered cab
ofile, the front of which was now made vertical in the
le elevation and wider at the top to enable slightly
ger front windows to be fitted to help improve
ibility.

The front-end casing has been squared-up and the now
standard cowl was fitted along with short smoke
deflectors.

Sanding has been added to the front and rear driving
wheels and the valance profile has been simplified.

100-gallon Tender - attached to second series when built

is series was built with a different profile and thicker
ates than the first series. Shown in full Southern
alachite livery.

e spring hangers have been changed, although the
les for the long hangers had already been drilled in
e frame. Rear raves were not provided, but the
atework was finished above the tender top, which was
ven a camber (indicated by a dotted line).

ont water fillers were fitted but were blanked off soon
ter entering service.

The side view shows the train heating pipe running
above the springs. The vacuum brake pipe ran on the
other side (see other drawings). Starting with this series
the footplate doors and fall plate were fitted to the
tender rather than the locomotive.

The part drawing shows the TIA tank fitted across the
tender top and the vacuum reservoirs have been stacked
in a pyramid to create the space required. The air pipe is
covered by a box to protect it.

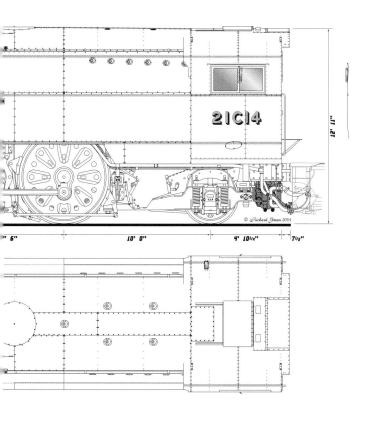

21C14

12' 11"

6" 10' 0" 4' 10¼" 7½"

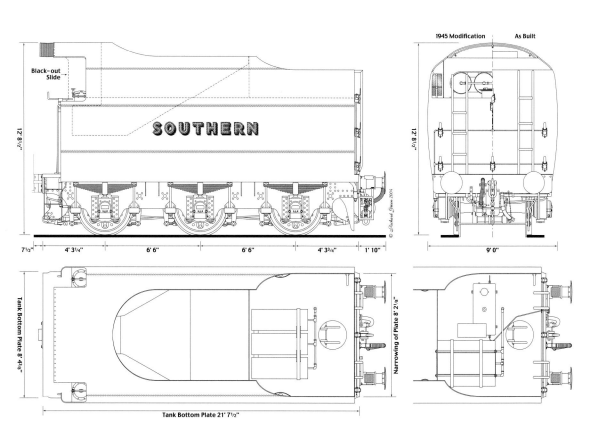

Black-out Slide

SOUTHERN

12' 8½"

7½" 4' 3¼" 6' 6" 6' 6" 4' 3¾" 1' 10"

1945 Modification   As Built

12' 8½"

9' 0"

Tank Bottom Plate 8' 4⅜"

Narrowing of Plate 8' 2⅛"

Tank Bottom Plate 21' 7½"

© Richard Green 2004

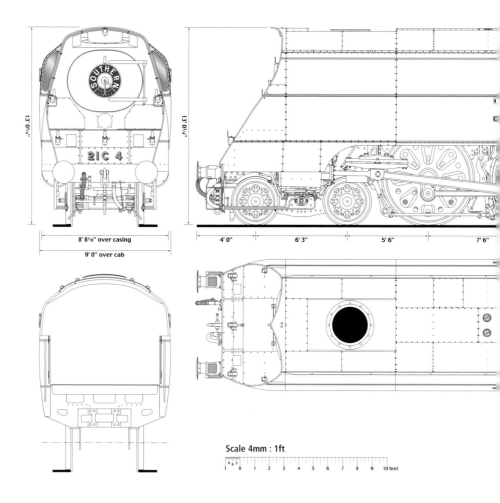

Scale 4mm : 1ft

First Series – 21C4 *Cunard White Star*

As named on 1 January in full Southern malachite livery with the initial smoke clearance modifications.

The valance over the coupled wheels has been cut back and the metal sheeting use for the casing on the first two locomotives has been replaced by Limpet board (an asbestos product) with a horizontal steel strengthening rib to save weight. Steel plates have been fitted to the cab side windows as a blackout precaution.

A small window, above the main windows on fireman's side, has been fitted to help illumination of the Detroit lubricator. Hinged doors have been provided in the boiler roof to aid access to the whistle and manifold isolating valves.

Note the enlarged 'C' in the engine's number.

5,000-gallon Tender - attached to first series when built

Shows the high back version for this series arrived at after experience with the two early tenders, in full Southern malachite livery.

The rear drawing shows a split view with the as built high backed version on the right and the 1944-45 cut down on the left. The top of the 5,000-gallon tender was flat with drainage holes near the bunker and front fillers.

Originally they were built with black-out curtains, which were later changed for metal slides. The filler is of a Maunsell pattern.

The part drawing shows the rear raves removed and TIA tank fitted. To gain space the vacuum reservoirs have been piled in a pyramid. The TIA air pipe is covered by a box to protect it from lumps of coal and heavy boots!

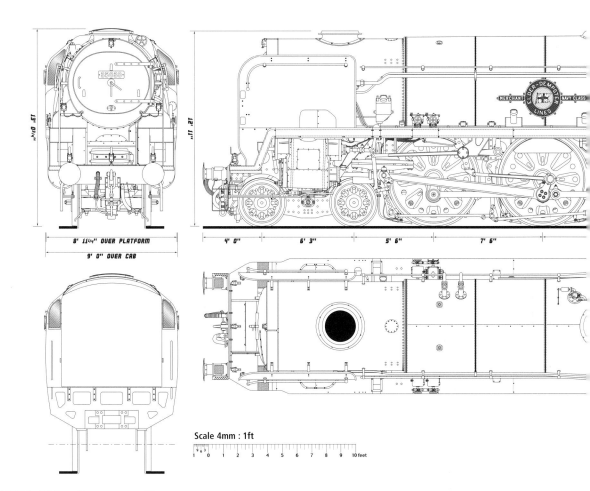

Scale 4mm : 1ft

...built – 35030 *Elder Dempster Lines*

...own as running in 1965.

...built in April 1958 to designs drawn up by R.G. Jarvis. ...e rebuilding removed the air-smoothed casing and ...placed Bulleid's enclosed valve gear with three sets of ...andard Walschaerts valve gear operated by a manual ...ew reverser. The smokebox was also replaced by a ...andard cylindrical type, but the Bulleid smokebox door ...as retained.

...nding was reinstated to the leading driver and the ...ar sander was turned to supply sand when running in

reverse. The height of the sand filling pipes varied across the class (see list on right).

Standard BR steam operated drain cocks (previously given trials on the 'Guinea Pig' locos, replaced Bulleid's manually operated ones.

The class were later fitted with AWS equipment (commencing in 1959) and speedometer (commencing in 1960).

Although rebuilt the locomotive remained 90% Bulleid!

...250/6,000-gallon Rebodied Tenders

...e to the bad condition of a number of first series ...dies new ones were constructed in the late 1950s to ...place them. Shown here in late BR livery.

...ey were built with the BR briquette system of water ...eatment, the container being situated between the ...ge rectangular fillers.

...e two vacuum cylinders were completely covered to ...p coal falling between them.

The routing of the vacuum and steam heating pipes was altered so that they went between the frames ahead of the guard iron, as on the third series tenders.

(Part drawing) When the coal weighing tender body needed replacing a stretched version was built with 2ft added at the back. A further difference from the 5,250 gallon version was the fitting of two round-topped ladders at the rear.

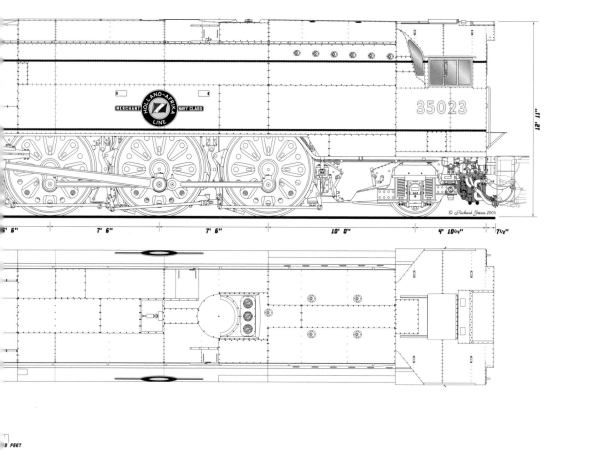

MERCHANT NAVY CLASS HOLLAND-AFRIKA LINE

35023

12' 11"

5' 6"　　　7' 6"　　　7' 6"　　　10' 0"　　　4' 10¼"　　7½"

© Richard Green 2004

10 FEET

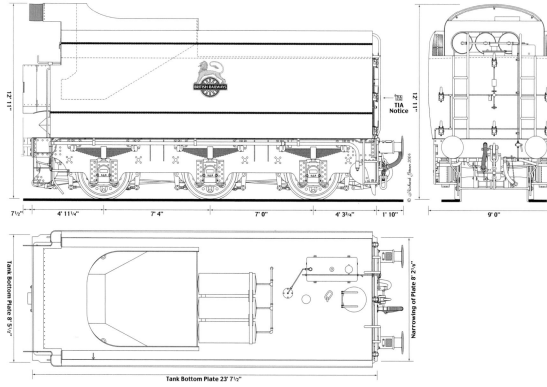

BRITISH RAILWAYS

TIA Notice

12' 11"

12' 11"

7½"　4' 11¼"　　7' 4"　　　7' 0"　　4' 3¾"　1' 10"

© Richard Green 2004

9' 0"

Tank Bottom Plate 8' 5½"

Narrowing of Plate 8' 2⅛"

Tank Bottom Plate 23' 7½"

Third Series –
35023 *Holland-Afrika Line*

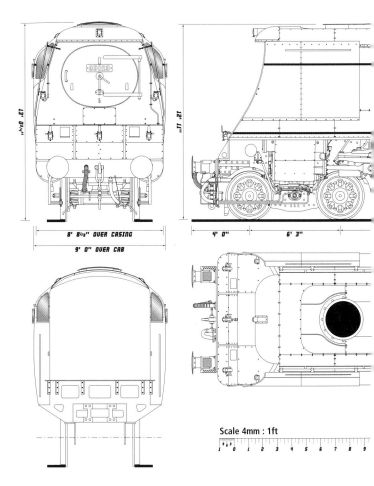

8' 8½" OVER CASING
9' 0" OVER CAB

4' 0"   6' 3"

Scale 4mm : 1ft

Shown in November 1954 after general overhaul and painted in BR green.

This series was built with the 1948 V-shaped fronted cab and had metal window frames fitted with the new standard three panes. Fabricated trailing trucks were used with a cover added to the top of the springs to stop the ingress of ash. The generator has been lowered below the cab sheeting. Larger smoke deflectors were fitted from new. The panel in front of the cylinders (fitted when built) has been removed to aid maintenance.

The major modification for this locomotive made at the general overhaul was the resiting of the safety valves to the rear of the dome (In the original position, water was occasionally discharged through the safety valves. This happened particularly when the locomotive was braking on a down gradient and at stations such as Winchester it was known for waiting passengers to be sprayed with water!). The resiting of the safety valves involved the repositioning of the pipe feeding the steam manifold and this, in turn, fouled the firebox front top washout plug. The remedy was to reposition the washout plug three inches to the right.

Other alterations included the replacement of the hinged doors for the whistle and manifold valves by sliding doors with grab handles, and the removal of the front sanding gear together with the blanking over of the sliding cover.

6,000-gallon Tender - attached to third series when built

The tenders built for the third series locomotive were longer to enable an increase in water capacity. Shown here in BR green with the large version of the Lion on Wheel crest.

They were fitted from new with TIA water treatment and owing to extra length of the tender top there was space available to fit it without resorting to stacking the vacuum tanks. In the mid-1950s, a notice was attached to the lighting conduit informing the locomotive's crew that the TIA was in use and the drawing shows this addition.

The vacuum pipe is routed above the springs, going between the frames ahead of the guard iron.

These tenders were fitted with LMS-type buffers.

The drainage holes from the tender top exited above the rear springs so a chute was provided to divert the water over the spring.

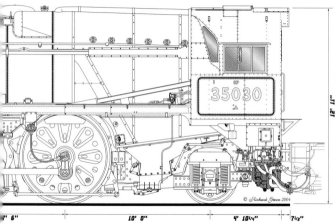

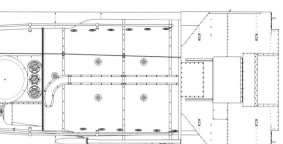

Sand Filling Pipes

Two short;	13, 14, 18, 20, 22, 25

Two long;	1, 2, 3, 4, 5, 6, 7, 8, 9, 24

The rest had one of each

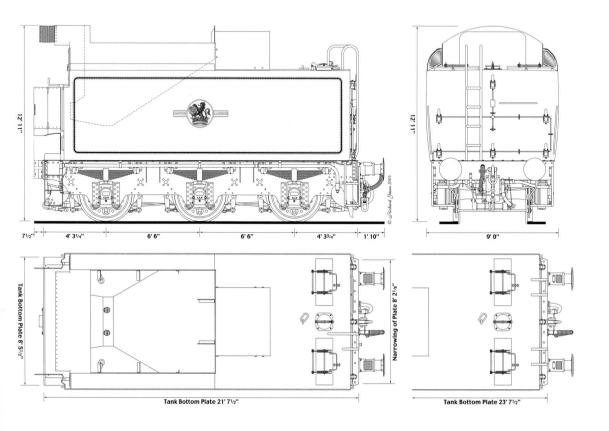

Publisher's Note

The drawing for the Second Series locomotives has been depicted with a First Series tender. The correct version is shown below. In producing this Addenda sheet the opportunity has been taken to complete the range of cut-down tender drawings.

5,100-gallon Tender — attached to second series when built

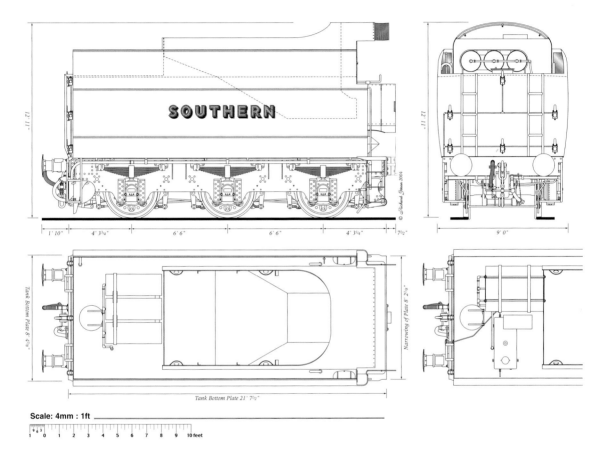

Scale: 4mm : 1ft

This series was built with a different profile and thicker plates than the first series. Shown in full Southern malachite livery.

The spring hangers have been changed, although the holes for the long hangers had already been drilled in the frame. Rear raves were not provided, but the platework was finished above the tender top, which was given a camber (indicated by a dotted line).

Front water fillers were fitted but were blanked off soon after entering service.

The side view shows the train heating pipe running above the springs. The vacuum brake pipe ran on the other side (see other drawings). Starting with this series the footplate doors and fall plate were fitted to the tender rather than the locomotive.

The part drawing shows the TIA tank fitted across the tender top and the vacuum reservoirs have been stacked in a pyramid to create the space required. The air pipe is covered by a box to protect it.

Note: The final sentence to the top caption on page 104 should read: The drawing also shows the earlier form of casing around the cylinders.

5,000-gallon Cut Down Tender

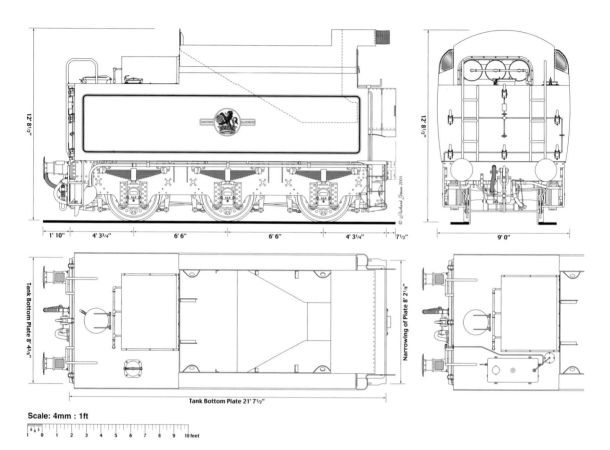

12' 8½"

1' 10"   4' 3¾"   6' 6"   6' 6"   4' 3¼"   7½"

12' 8½"

9' 0"

Tank Bottom Plate 8' 4¾"

Narrowing of Plate 8' 2⅞"

Tank Bottom Plate 21' 7½"

Scale: 4mm : 1ft

1 0 1 2 3 4 5 6 7 8 9 10 feet

Shows the first series tender cut down and fitted with BR briquette water treatment system in late BR livery.

The high sides have been cut away and fire iron tunnels have been welded to the top of the tank. These appeared to attempt to follow the profile of the later series tenders — some more successful than others!

The vacuum cylinders have been covered, but left exposed at the back.

The routing of the vacuum and steam heating pipes were altered so they went between the frames ahead of the guard iron, as on the third series tenders. The springs hangers were changed to those of the second and third series. The ladders have square top stiles on the outside and a foot catch is fitted to the filler cap.

The part drawing shows the earlier TIA water treatment fitted alongside the vacuum reservoirs.

5,100-gallon Cut Down Tender

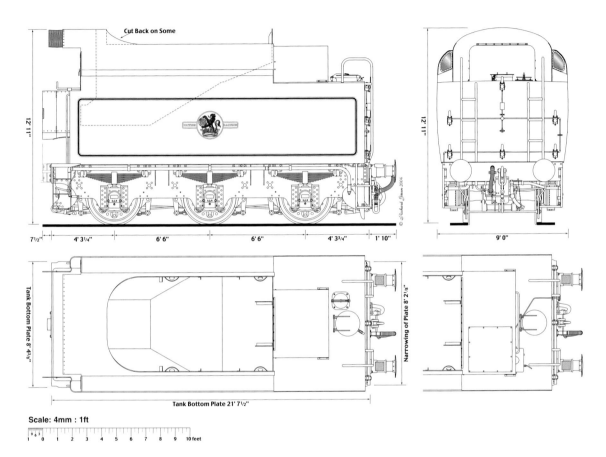

Cut Back on Some

12' 11"

7½" 4' 3¼" 6' 6" 6' 6" 4' 3¾" 1' 10"

12' 11"

9' 0"

Tank Bottom Plate 8' 4⅜"

Narrowing of Plate 8' 2⅛"

Tank Bottom Plate 21' 7½"

Scale: 4mm : 1ft

1 0 1 2 3 4 5 6 7 8 9 10 feet

Shows the second series tender cut down and fitted with BR briquette water treatment system in late BR livery.

The high sides have been cut down and fire iron tunnels produced by welding a cover between the side and the coal bunker.

The vacuum reservoirs have been replaced by two larger ones, placed centrally and completely covered.

The routing of the vacuum and steam heating pipes was altered to go between the frames ahead of the guard iron, as on the third series tenders. The ladders

have square top stiles on the outside and a foot catch is fitted to the filler cap.

The part drawing shows the earlier version with TIA water treatment fitted. The vacuum cylinders were fitted on the right-hand side and the TIA tank projected from the back on the left-hand side with a gap above to allow filling.

Note that when the handrail tops were fitted to the stiles, the TIA container required moving further inside the protecting cover.

6,000-gallon Cut Down Tender

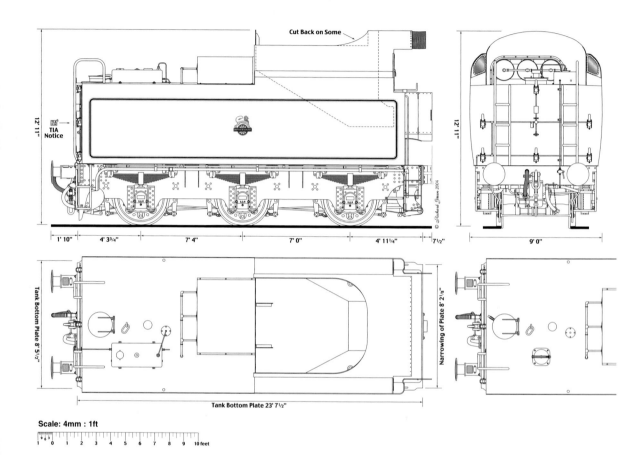

Scale: 4mm : 1ft

Shows the third series tender cut down and fitted with TIA water treatment system in early BR livery with standard size lion on wheel crest.

The high sides have been cut down and fire iron tunnels produced by welding a cover between the side and the coal bunker.

The vacuum reservoir cylinders have been covered but left exposed at the back. The water drains can be now be clearly seen on the tank top.

The ladders have been fitted with square top stiles on the outside.

The part drawing shows the later BR briquette water treatment system and a foot catch fitted to the filler cap. The TIA pressure fitting is still in place but blanked off.